Reaching The Beyond

Reaching The Beyond

DEAN C. GARDNER

Ordering Information:

For orders and inquiries, please contact:
1-888-404-1388
www.goldtouchpress.com
book.orders@goldtouchpress.com

Printed in the United States of America

Dedicated to Alexandre Vashakmadze,
a young master and artisan.

Contents

SECTION 1

A Time in Space

To have a muse
And be someone's dream
How Hope Shields
Accelerates
Through being
And nothingness
Taking what is there
And turning it
Into a beauteous wonder.

So
She is an artist
Configuring
The close at hand
Into the splendor
Of the beyond.

How
Having a muse
Liberates her
From the constraints
Of phenomenal
Reality
Allowing her
To transform Truth
Into the face
Of becoming there.

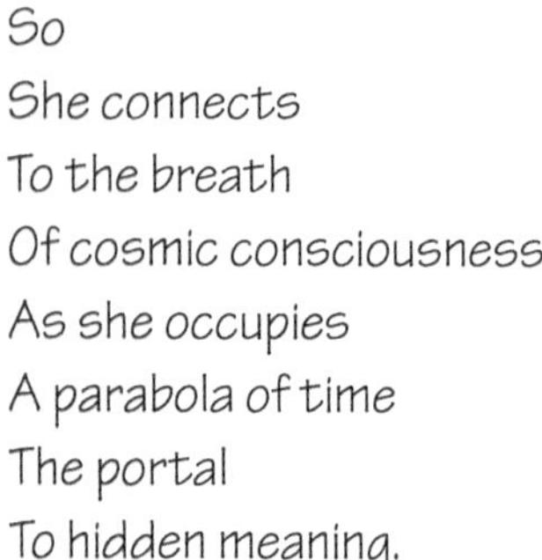

So
She connects
To the breath
Of cosmic consciousness
As she occupies
A parabola of time
The portal
To hidden meaning.

Then
As Winchester's dream
She sees
The substance
Of time and times
And a half
Undressing Truth
From the shroud
Of the dull round.

How
The muscle
Of Truth forms
The fearful symmetry
Of becoming there
And The Unknown God
Adopts her
As one of promise.

In the grasp
Of her muse
She finds the rhythm
That defines the music
Of what matters.

So
She is his dream
And he is her muse.

With the flow
Of the duduk, the artists
Grabowski
Vashakmadze and Shields
Opened becoming there
To the deep touch
Until the dull round
Exploded
With beauty and wonder.

It was
That they tapped
The interstices
Of time and space
Imaging the connection
Between self
And the other
As a parable of Truth.

At the brink
Of nothingness
Each drew the breath
Of free will
As the music of eternity
Infused a calling
Within the heart.

Driven
By the acceptance
Of destiny
They worked their magic
With urgency
Because linear time
Governed
Their biological clock.

Times
And times and a half
Presented moments
When the artists
Moved
To the palm
At the end of mind.

Then
They became the landscape
Of always and forever.

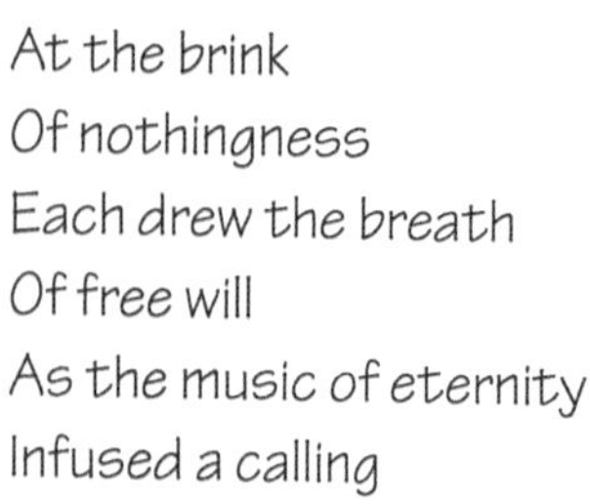

So
There was Hope
In the land
Of the free
And brave
And there was
Her muse
Inspiring her
Onto always and forever.

As she shifted
To a parabola
Of time
The skies witnessed
An epiphany
Of Truth
And she read
The signs
Of the now.

Moments flourished
Rich in their design
With the deep touch
And Winchester
Devoted himself
To her pleasure.

As she danced
To the music
Of being and time

Freedom
Reached into mind
And the walls
Of self-deception
Crumbled into dust.

How
The earth moved
Ever closer
To glory
As she journeyed
Through trance
And time and space
Celebrated
With the all
Of her substance.

Then
She explored
The unknown
Seeking hidden meaning
Finding
Cosmic consciousness
As the source
Of ideation.

So
She bathed
In the moment
Of victory

And her muse declared her
As the deep touch of passion.

So
The bells tell
The hour
And Hope listens
To the call
Of the wilds
As she gathers
Times
Into moments
Redeemed.

Then
She uncovers
A secret
Buried in hidden
Meaning
And visions
Of a house
Of many mansions
Appears in the sky.

It is
A golden edifice
Timeless in its stand.

How
She removes
Times of trial
With her graceful
Smile
Kissing the sky
Of forevermore.

So
The hour emerges
Into destiny
As she feeds
On Truth
And she accepts
Her place in mind.

To unearth meaning
To probe the unknown
To touch understanding
How
She is filled
As destiny's child
And Winchester holds
His precious Hope
Close to his heart.

So
She rubs becoming there
With the fragrance
Of cosmic consciousness

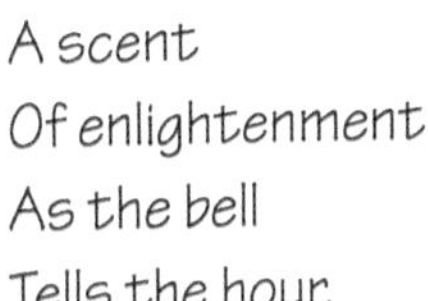

A scent
Of enlightenment
As the bell
Tells the hour.

How
Truth comes
From the spirit
Of what matters.

Jetting
Through time
And space
The persona
Of being and nothingness
Rode his hog
His dream embracing
The moment.

The road led them
Into the deep
Of magic
Where freedom let loose
Screaming thunder.

How
Eternity awoke
In the blood

Of becoming there
As his dream
Squeezed space
Into a parabola
Of time.

Her raven hair
And blue eyes
Lit the way
To a moment
Of pure passion..

Then
They entered
An atom of thought
Reaching the authentic
Article
As they traveled
Across a bridge
To epiphany.

So
Each moment
On the road
Exploded
Into an arrangement
Of colors
Defining the substance
Of what mattered.

So
The love
Of the open road
And the love of a dream
Was enough
To liberate her
From the bondage
Of the here and now.

To go
Beyond space and time
They pursued
The moment of Truth.

His name is
Winchester
And he dwells
In the deep touch.

She is
Hope Shields
And she configures
The substance
Of becoming there.

In her third eye
Rolling thunder
Expressed
The blind want
In her heart
As the drums
Of eternity ponded
Purpose
Into becoming there.

Although passion had
A hold on her
She heard
The whispers
Of hidden meaning
Falling from the shadows
But she embraced
The calling
Of The Counselor.

As an image
Grew
Into the unfolding
Of being and time
She pursued thought
As a still life
Orchestrating
The presence of Truth.

It was
A landscape of mind
Entangled
With a wilderness
Uncovered by her trance.

It was
The design
Of a self-portrait
Colored with scarlet.

How
The deep touch
Of The Word
Shaped
What was there
Into a lament
Of the duduk.

To sing
In the presence
Of The Unknown God:
How
Hope wept with thanks.

They were in pursuit
Of The Unknown God
While the scars

From the past
Left marks
Of painful wandering.

Deep inside
Winchester grew
The desire for purpose
As he followed
The road to Truth.

Without purpose
He is a dry
Angry man
And it is
From his dream
His true love
That he found hope.

She is
The lamp
In the open air
That shines
Through the darkness.

So
The road led
Through the wilderness
Of Tennessee
A beginning of times
And a half.

There
He saw the substance
Of becoming there
As he looked
Into the face
Of the wind.

As mind traveled
Into the beyond
He touched
The rudiments
Of the authentic article
Spoken to him
From the wilds.

In the trees
And mountains
Spoke the voice
Of eternity
And he listened
Carefully
As he rode his hog
Onto forevermore.

In the forests
And mountains
Spoke the voice
Of eternity.

How
His dream loves him.

At the edge
Of the Tennessee River
They stopped
And walked
To the water's edge.

There
A vision swept
Across the here and now
And Winchester
Launched
Into the beyond.

He saw
A house of many
Mansions
And it glowed
Through time and space.

It was
A moment
When the sound
Of drums

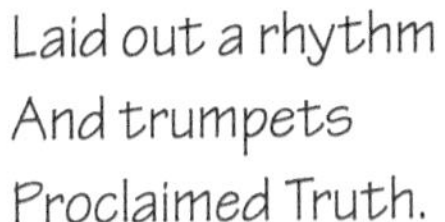

Laid out a rhythm
And trumpets
Proclaimed Truth.

So
This is the home
Of peace
Beyond understanding.

Waves of joy
Rose
Across becoming there
And his dream
Held silence
In her heart.

Then
The vision stretched
Into times and a half
As thunder
Exploded in his mind.

It was
A moment when
Winchester
Felt the deep touch
Of eternity.

It was
A moment when
All and everything
Entered
A vertical column
Of time.

How
Glorious the sight
Of cosmic consciousness
As being and time
Defined
What mattered.

Then
Winchester, driven to be
sat
On the mercy seat.

In times and a half
Hope ventured
Into the unknown
Spiriting
What was there
After probing
Being and nothingness.

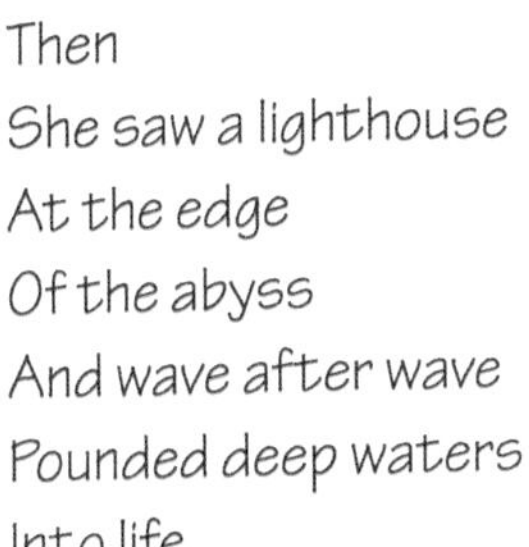

Then
She saw a lighthouse
At the edge
Of the abyss
And wave after wave
Pounded deep waters
Into life.

So
There was the expanse
Where hidden meaning
Dwelt
And Shields took
Its secrets
Into the core
Of her substance.

How
The other side
Of becoming there
Painted an overture
To what mattered
As Winchester
Fueled
Her passion
For adventure.

It was
That she celebrated
Her connection

To cosmic consciousness
With the belief
In The Unknown God
As mind leaped
From the shadows
Of the dull round.

Then
the image
of the other
brought Truth
into heart
and The Word gave
breath
to her trance.

How
Eternity fed
The moment
With wonder
As time and space
Filled the light
Of becoming.

So
It was the beacon
Of Truth
That she followed.

So
There was
A connection
Between Winchester
And cosmic consciousness
Set by the third eye.

So
The minute particular
Triggered
Wave upon wave
Of images onto mind
As he probed the unknown
For Truth.

Then
A figure stepped
Into the light
And he wore
A camel-hair-robe
With a leather belt.

He lived on honey
And locusts.

His life pointed to The Word.

To believe
What is there
As Truth

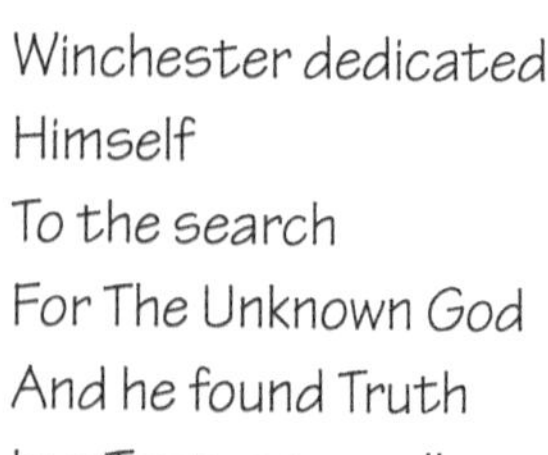

Winchester dedicated
Himself
To the search
For The Unknown God
And he found Truth
In a Tennessee valley.

Then
The earth opened
Its treasure chest
And a plethora
Of Truth filled
Becoming there.

So
Time past lived
In the mind
As self traveled
Through being and time.

So
All and everything
Lived in the past
As time present
Suspended possibility
In the interstices
Of mind.

Then
A moment awakened
Passage
To a vertical column of time.

There
Cosmic consciousness
Dwells.

Mounting her hog
Hope set out
To discover the secrets
Carried by the wind
And Winchester followed .

Fusing becoming there
With the beyond
They came to a portal
That took them
Into the body
Of cosmic consciousness.

There
They climbed
Into things in themselves
And a mystery tree
Presented itself
On a barren hill.

It was
The place of the skull
As time
Eclipsed the sun
And they dismounted
Their hogs
Leaving linear time
And its constraints.

Then
Time past opened
The moment.

Then
Blessed assurance
Filled them
With a vision of peace
Beyond understanding.

Then
The wind blew
Eternity
Into their hearts.

So
They saw the gift
From The Unknown God.

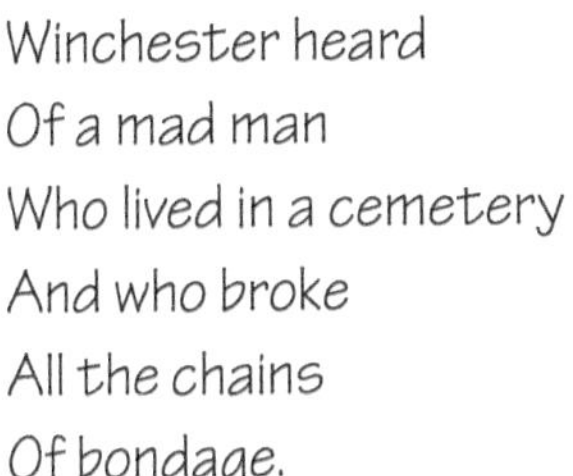

Winchester heard
Of a mad man
Who lived in a cemetery
And who broke
All the chains
Of bondage.

Living among demons
Nothing
Could hold him down.

Winchester looked
For this man
Because one day
He became
Right
In his mind
Leaving the cemetery
To live a right life.

So
Time and times
And a half
Passed
As thoughts
Carried
A meaning linked
To possibility
But to believe
In the thoughts

Of the other
How
Truth demanded a leap
Of faith
And Winchester
Was not ready
For that step.

Then
He was on the road
Passing
Through time and space
As his dream
Held onto his life.

They followed
The light of Truth
As they approached
A parabola of time
And the juxtaposition
Of things in themselves
Led
To everywhere.

To search
For meaning
When all was askew
How
He yearned
To right his life

Although it seemed
Wandering
Was his destiny.

The time came
When Hope Shields
Mounted
Her own hog
And she rode
The frontier
With passion.

She
Loved the freedom
Of riding
The rush of the wind
Across her body.

So
She and Winchester
Looked
To the calculus
Of becoming there
The figures
Of time and space.

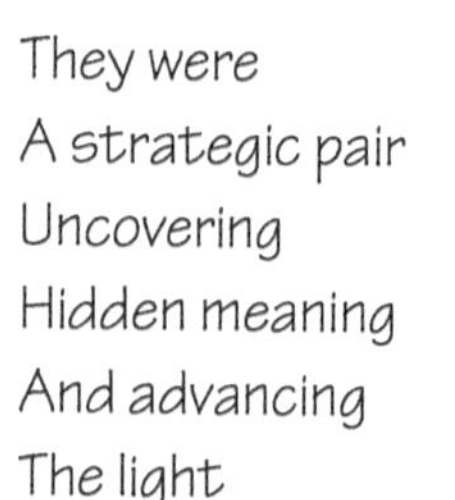

They were
A strategic pair
Uncovering
Hidden meaning
And advancing
The light
Of understanding.

It was
That riding
Through the straights
Of eternity
Enriched them
With the power
Of cosmic consciousness
As the road
Transfixed meditation
On The Unknown God.

How
Truth was in
The wind
As they probed
A parabola
Of time
From their anchor
In flesh and blood.

There was
A music
In the wilderness
That infused them
With a connection
To The Word
As the thunder
From their motors
Trumped
Times and times
And a half.

So
Truth flourished
On the road
With the liberty
To be.

Surrounded
By the other
In a coffee shop
Winchester and his dream
Found distance to becoming there.

It was
The existence
Of the other

That pointed
To the nothingness
Inside him.

A hollow dwelt inside him.

In a sense
It was being
A lone wolf
That took him
Into the quest
For The Unknown God.

He knew
That from somewhere
He would find
The deep touch
Of what mattered.

So
It was meaninglessness
Meaninglessness
That held him tightly
And its hold
Was unforgiving.

On a lamppost
A crow sat
Calling to the sky
For Truth

As Winchester listened
To things
In-themselves.

It was
His heart beating
Moments
Of nothingness
That took him
To the other side
Of being and time
And Winchester
Searched for his place
In eternity.

How
In a sense
The quest
For The Unknown God
Was his third eye.

So
The moon was round
And full
As spirits gathered
In the bones
Of phenomenal reality.

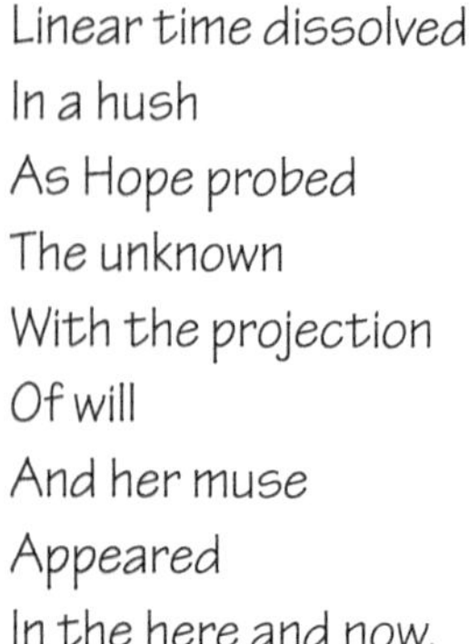

Linear time dissolved
In a hush
As Hope probed
The unknown
With the projection
Of will
And her muse
Appeared
In the here and now.

It was
The substance
Of his mirrored image
That moved her
Into deep trance
As darkness filled
With spirits
Of being and time.

Once there
The blood
Of the celestial clocks
Constituted
The moment
As the moon shone
Upon the tombstones
Of time past.

So
In the hollow
Of becoming there
Hope spear-headed
The advance of Truth
From the ashes
Of phenomenal reality
Into the brilliance
Of cosmic consciousness.

Then
A trumpet sounded
And spirits
Moved into mind.

How
The darkness
And the shadows
Of darkness
Left Hope Shields
Because
The sun also rises.

So
She laid it on the line
For her muse
With the passion
Of the moment.

SECTION 2

Entering the Crawl Space

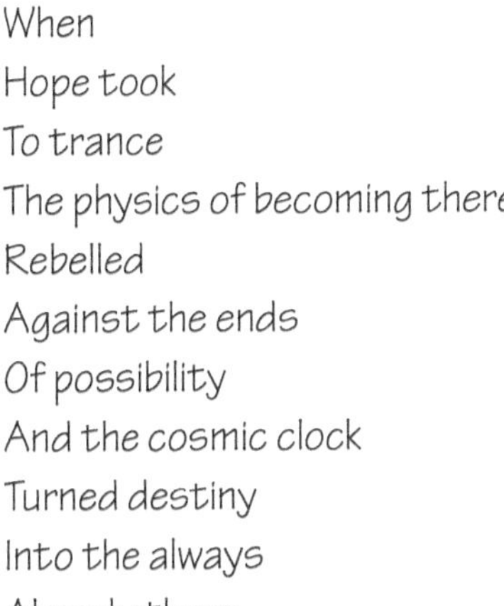

When
Hope took
To trance
The physics of becoming there
Rebelled
Against the ends
Of possibility
And the cosmic clock
Turned destiny
Into the always
Already there.

In that moment
Her free spirit
Launched
Into the muscle
Of want
As she followed
The shadows of desire.

To grasp the message
From the unknown
She traced the steps
Through the beyond
Where the secrets
Of time and space
Whispered
The bones of Truth.

How
The will
Of the flesh
Seizes possibility
And dreams
Carry the weight
Of what matters.

Stirring the mind
Into the song of eternity
Hope followed
The rhythm
Of passion and heart.

So
Her third eye
Opened
And treasures filled her
With the deep touch
Consummating
Times and a half
In a parabola of time.

While mind
Plummets into the void
Hope battles
With nothingness

Ands her heart listens
For the calling in the wind.

How
She longs
For the deep touch.

Across the sky
Flew a crow
And at her feet
Sparrows
Hunted for crumbs.

At her table
Vashakmadzze drew
The light
Of the everlasting
Dwelling in the look
Of his love
As a two
Dimenbsional reality
Depicted
The birth of Truth.

A song
Erupted from his heart
That lifted
Hope
Into a horizon
Where beauty shone

As a brilliant moment
And mind found
Its way to the other side.

So
Love redeems time past.

So
Life goes on
In the garden
Of tables and chairs.

Cloaked in darkness
Times and a half
Shadow
The movement
Of becoming there
While an eerie odor
Brings death
To life.

The seed of eternity
Planted in mind
That broke light
Into the moment
And the celestial clocks
Opened the authentic article
To the artist in Hope.

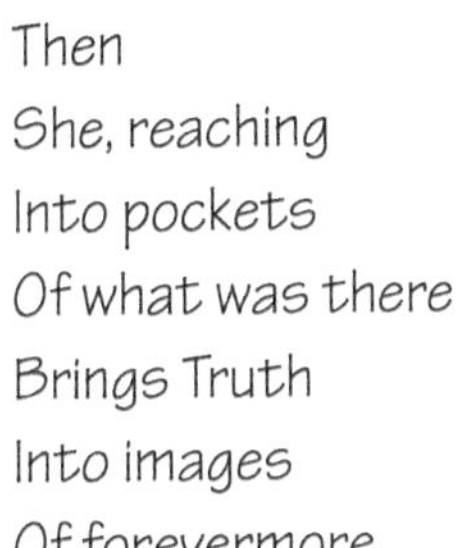

Then
She, reaching
Into pockets
Of what was there
Brings Truth
Into images
Of forevermore.

From the unknown
Cosmic consciousness
Brought life
Revealing the ends
Of possibility
While mind painted
A parabola of time.

Then
Hope, reaching
Into thought
Danced
To the song
Of the duduk
As the breath
Of The Unknown God
Filled her
With the drive
To be
Beyond mind.

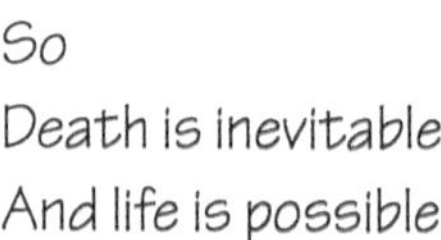

So
Death is inevitable
And life is possible.

So
There is
The resurrection of the dead.

How
The Word is
The greatest teacher.

Hope and Winchester
Were sitting
At a table
In the garden
Of tables and chairs
When an artist
Vashakmadze
Showed up.

He is
A kindred spirit
With rare
Conceptual capability.

He may be
On the cutting edge
Of postmodernism.

So
They shared
Some time and space
With a clear
Vision of Truth
As they occupied
The authentic article
Together.

They understood
That the word
Reality by itself
Had lost its meaning
So they engaged
Their anchor
Into the heart
Of phenomenal reality
As a touchstone
To the beyond.

Near by
Was an old man
With his blue guitar
And his music
Took them into another
World.

It was
The articulation
Of the blue guitar
That carried them
Through being
And nothingness
As they set
Milestones
In a parabola
Of time.

Then
They beheld
The face of eternity
As Truth grew
Into heart and mind.

Shields
A dazzling beauty
Wooed her muse
With the passion
Found
In the heart
Of love
And in the wilds
Of the purple mountains
Majesty.

Together
They explored
Phenomenal reality
Establishing meaning
From the close at hand
And then launching
Into the unknown
Where the spirits
Of the authentic article
Dwelled.

So
They mounted
Their hogs
Believing themselves
Into the realm
Of celestial clocks
And escaping
From the dull round.

How
The road radiated
With amazement
Taking them
Into a portal
That led them
Deep
Into the beyond.

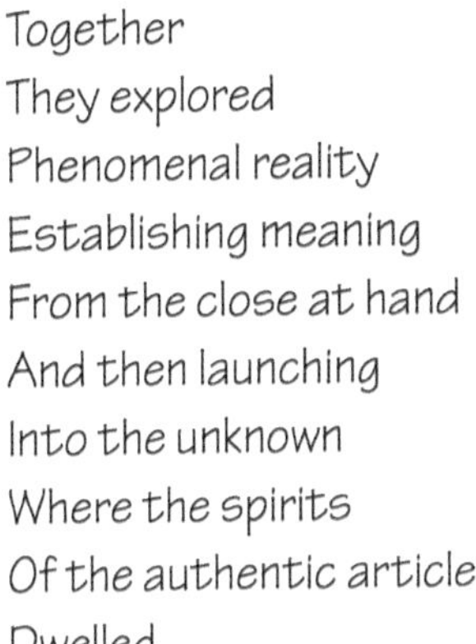

Time and space
Exploded
As they ventured
Through being
And nothingness
And once there
They entwined
Themselves
With the sweat
Of desire.

How
The music
Of eternity presented
An image
Of their shadows
And together they found
A private joy
An epiphany
Onto forevermore.

Then
They consummated
Truth
In the reaches
Of their devotion
As Shields
Visited his dreams

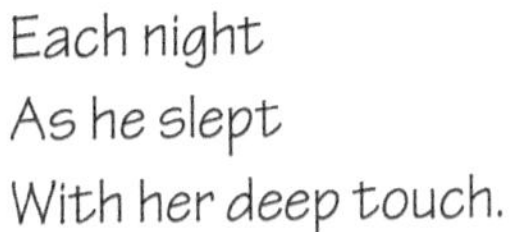

Each night
As he slept
With her deep touch.

So
Vashakmadze
Orchestrated a self
Portrait
At his easel
As the hard lines
Of light and dark
Encompassed his stand.

So
There was the organic
And inorganic
Portraying life
In the moment
While he held
His brush
Before the living
Canvas.

How
He took form
And substance
Into patterns

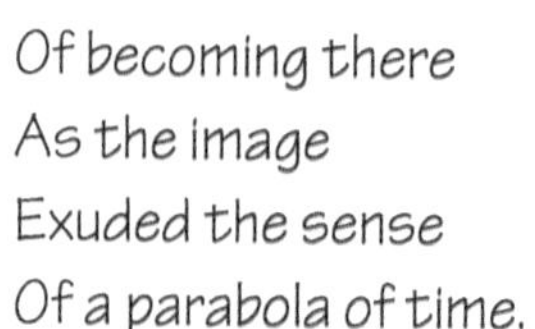

Of becoming there
As the image
Exuded the sense
Of a parabola of time.

It was
A moment extracted
From time
And times and a half.

From the distance
The echo of a duduk
Spirited
His passion
As he fashioned
The connection
To cosmic consciousness
From phenomenal
Reality.

Upon seeing
What was there
Mind
Slipped into the beyond
And understanding
Prospered
Because a portal
Opened
To the unknown
With the lamp

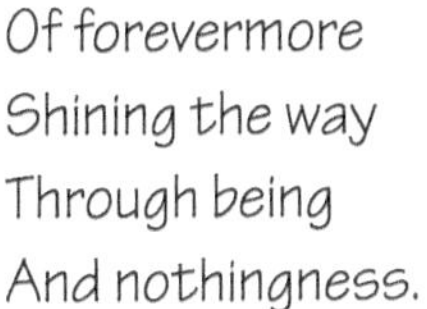

Of forevermore
Shining the way
Through being
And nothingness.

So
Vashakmadze
Possessed
A clear vision
Of phenomenal reality
As an access
To Truth.

So
Vashakmadze
Believed himself
Into the architecture
Of hidden meaning
And the treasure
Of Truth.

Once there
He beheld
The house of many
Mansions.

Then
The magic
Of the deep touch
Centered
The moment
Upon the beyond
As Hope emerged
From the wilderness.

There was
A song in her heart
And vision in her mind.

Winchester
Her muse
Moved mountains
Into the air
With a will composed
From the always
Already there
As a trumpet
Sounded
The advent
Of times and a half.

How
Truth reaches
Becoming there
Summoning service
To The Unknown God.

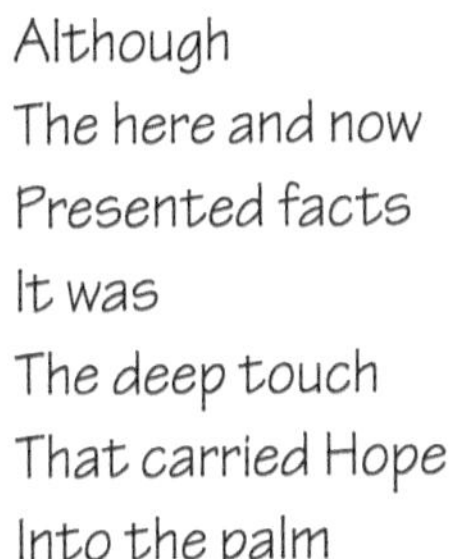

Although
The here and now
Presented facts
It was
The deep touch
That carried Hope
Into the palm
At the end of mind.

To love Truth
And to serve
The Word
Brought an opening
To the other side
Of a parabola of time.

Once there
She felt the spirits
Of what mattered
With the hearkening
Of life itself.

So
There was the trace
To cosmic consciousness
With each breath
A trigger
Inducing meditation.

Then
Truth does not
Occupy
The close at hand
But the close at hand
Is the channel
To Truth.

When a bolt
Of light struck
The heart
Of being and time
Two angels joined
An artist
At a table
In the garden
As a thick fog
Drifted in.

An elegant smile
Captured the moment.

Sketching
A river of thought
With the deep
Of the water
Fathoming the wonder

Inside the wonder
Inside time and space
Grabowski formed
The deep touch.

In the shallows
Of becoming there
He faced the void
As the sky shed tears
Ands the angels
Took him
Into the center
Of the other side.

There
A woman in a room
With her face
On the wall
With three eyes
Pulled time
Out of the void
And into Truth
As the moment endured
Onto forevermore
Liberating
Mind from the abyss.

How
The angels readied
His heart
For the everlasting.

Growing ever deeper
Into trance
Shields passed over
Being and nothingness
As she followed
The moon
Into the celestial
Clocks.

No longer was there
Past
Present or future
As the moment
Suspended time
As she felt
Her way
Through the interstices
Of phenomenal reality.

Then
An image appeared
In the waters

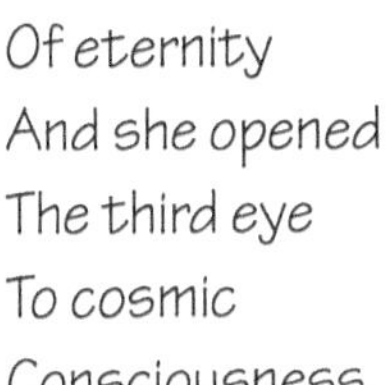

Of eternity
And she opened
The third eye
To cosmic
Consciousness.

Composing
What was there
Her biological clock
Kept time
With times
And a half.

Although
She could alter
Being and time
Her biological clock
Stayed steady
As a two-dimensional
Reality
Carried her
From milestone
To milestone.

There
In her view
Came a pond
With lily pads
And sunshine

A serene scene
To meditate upon.

Then
From waters
Of eternity
Emerged her muse
Wearing the armor
Of forevermore
And she embraced him
With the passion
In the spirit
Of beauty.

How
Hope found
Truth
In the waters
Of Winchester's desire.

So
She composed the will
Of the deep touch.

With the boiling of passion
In his blood, Hope visited
Winchester's dreams

That night
And he yielded to her will.

It was
The rub
Of flesh upon flesh
That took him
Into the wilds
Of her blue eyes
As his heart trumpeted
In an explosion
Of wonder.

Penetrating his dreams
Her sweat
Saturated becoming there
With desire.

So
Hope took him
With her deep touch
Opening him
To the throbbing rhythm
Of cosmic consciousness
As want eclipsed
His meat.

Her muse heated
In the moment
As his dreams

Carried him
Into the magic
Of her look.

So
She gave his dreams
The signature
Of her flesh
And he looked
Through her third eye
To see love
Forevermore.

Then
There was a calling
From the unknown
That planted
A vision
Of a child
In the darkness
Of a cave.

Hope had
No understanding of it
As her mind
Reached out
As a crow

Barked a signal
In being and time.

Then
Shadows consumed
The child
And a one-dimensional
Reality
Pounded Truth
Into the moment.

So
The magic
Of that time
Poured a warning
That trespass
Would not be
Allowed.

So
There in the cave
Was writing
On the wall
In a language
Understood
By silence.

How
Meaning escapes
From the other side

As cosmic
Consciousness
Infuses mind
With the deep touch.

Then
A portal eases
Into the moment
As the third eye
Opens to Truth
And Shields reads
Silence
A venture
Into thought.

How
Hungry the mind
In the face
Of hidden meaning.

How
The wilderness
Of becoming there
Confounds
The vision of Truth.

With a two
Dimensional reality
Vashakmadze expressed
The magic
Of being and time
As the celestial clocks
Moved the moment
Into becoming.

Shields was there
And so were
Seurat and van Gogh
Their laughter
Carrying
The authentic article.

From their third eye
Grew the connection
To cosmic consciousness
While an old soldier
Sat across the way
With desolation
In his bones.

Deep into nothingness
Mind sank
Into the void
The abyss swallowing
Him whole.

Then
A younger woman

And a thin smile
Creased his face
Although his eyes
Shone with the darkness
Of terror.

Because the wounds
Of time past
Never healed
The old soldier
Outlived himself
A certain tragedy.

He no longer had
Blood in his veins
Only tears
Although he could
Smile.

Vashakmadze captured
The moment.

In the muscle
Of Truth
Time present presents

Phenomenal reality
As The Unknown God
Pours the living moment
Into becoming.

So
What is there
Bleeds into the past
While the moment
By moment provides
Being and time.

The thin vapor
Of now recedes
As cosmic consciousness
Infuses the will
To be
With the drive
To eternity.

It is
That the artist
In Hope
Forms a moment
Where Truth dwells
Uncovering
The close at hand
As a step
Into forevermore
With each step

A longing
For what matters.

So
Shields provides
A testament
To the adventure
Of becoming.

How
The moment reveals
The way to Truth.

So
Life is indefinable
While living proceeds.

So
Her muse sized
Being and time
With the whip
Of will
As Hope
Spun the moment
With reaches
Of passion.

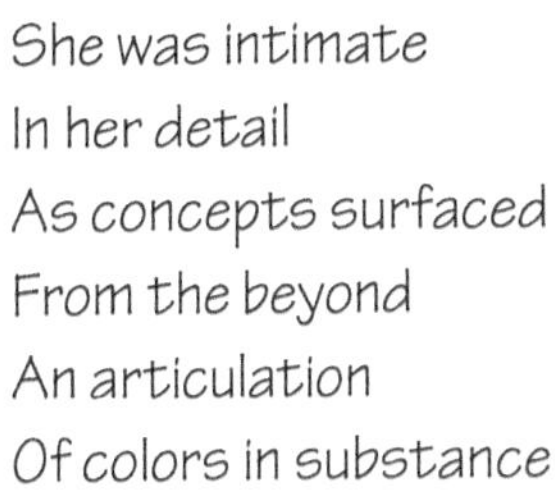

She was intimate
In her detail
As concepts surfaced
From the beyond
An articulation
Of colors in substance
And form.

Wearing the red badge
Of courage
She faced the abyss
As she painted
An image
That transcended
Linear time.

So
What was there
Shone
With the light
Of Truth
As her muse released
A frontier
Of possibility.

How
Truth shaped
What was there
As she took
To the unknown

Shedding the mask
Of self-deception.

Then
A crown of thorns
Marked
The beginning
Of a new age
Fashioned for those
Who are the chosen
Children.

So
To behold Truth
Uncovers the way
To commune
With The Unknown God.

In the physics
Of becoming there
Cosmic consciousness
Affixes linear time
To the song of eternity.

To hear
The birth pains
Of the now
Reveals the source

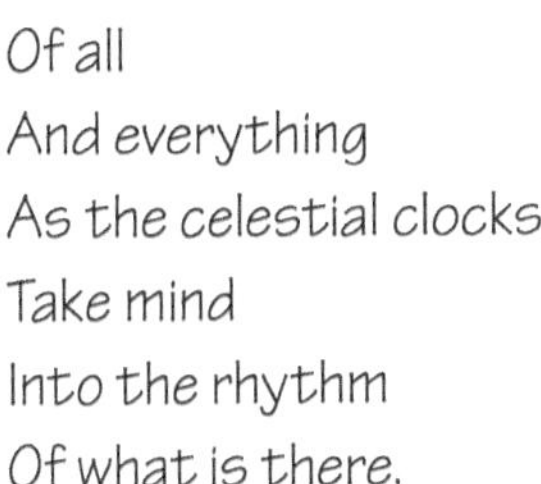

Of all
And everything
As the celestial clocks
Take mind
Into the rhythm
Of what is there.

Then
While in trance
Hope configures Truth
Into a moment
Of the always
Already there.

Although the unknown
Surrounds
The substance of self
With forms of thought
The artist pulls
Images
Of time and space
Into a para bola of time.

Although the expanse
Blurs her vision
With the multitude
She focuses
Upon the minute particular
For the look of Truth
In the given.

It is
That phenomenal reality
An infinite emanation
Of Truth, reaches
Into the physics
Of becoming there
Liberating thought.

While Hope gathered
The ends of possibility
A crow joined her
In the garden
Of tables and chairs
And eternity looked
Through her third eye.

While cosmic consciousness
Introduced the moment
To the authentic
Article
Hope grew
Into the magic of becoming there.

Then
The crow undressed
The substance of heart.

Then
The algorithm
Of possibility
Moved
The wilderness of thought
Into a view
Belonging to the physics
Of Truth.

It was
A vision of a wicker chair
And a pipe.

Then
The crow flew
Into a hole in the sky
Leaving a trace
To forevermore.

So
The crow left nothingness
As the mystery of possibility.

Hiding in the fog
The mountains whispered
The living moment into becoming there
As magic stirred
In her blood.

Shields drew a message
That liberated mind
Pulling heart
Into the center
Of things
In themselves.

Then
From the vast regions
Of nothingness
Came the rhythm of drums
And the cry of the duduk.

To stare
Into the jaws of the abyss
Shields tightly held
Her blessed assurance
Advancing steadily
Into the unknown.

Well into the deep
She took the blade
Of Truth
Striking light
Into what was there.

Times passed
And the mountains
Danced

Into the sky
As the fog retreated.

So
Her trance revealed
The signature
Of the deep touch
The drive of passion
Onto forevermore.

So
The substance
Of her meat traced
A wilderness of wonder.

As rain filled
The darkness
Magic circled becoming there
And time poured
Into silence.

There was
A throbbing
In the muscle
Of mind
While Hope placed
The signature
Of the authentic

Article
On the moment.

Bleeding in the rain
Her muse awakened
In pain
Because destiny
Blinded Truth
In the shadows
Of nothingness.

How
The figure
Of war
Fastened horror
Into a child
As a scream penetrated
Time and space.

So
Shields picked up
The banner of Truth
Charging into battle
While infused with the power
Of cosmic consciousness.

Then
The movement
Of the celestial clocks
Pulled the face

Of hidden meaning
Into phenomenal reality
As spirits fought
For the freedom
Known in Truth.

How
The language
Of the unknown
Ruptured thought.

How
The message
Of the unknown
Shattered mind.

So
Hope redefines
What is there
Into the image
Of form and substance
Speaking in wonder
And magic.

So
Magic is
What people can do
And miracles are
What The Unknown God
Does.

The traffic
Of here and now
Saturated the moment
As the race
Of nothingness
Occupied the minds
Of meaninglessness.

So
The other seemed
Blind
To the messages
Of eternity
As Winchester strained
To catch
The drift of a thing
In-itself.

To focus
On the minute
Particular
The fearsome
Symmetry
Of the now
Liberated him
From the constraints
Of self-deception.

His heart was pure
And his mind was clear.

In a sense
The search
For The Unknown God
Was his purpose
To gather meaning
In his life
His destiny.

It was not
He did not think
Himself
Greater than the others
Because they seemed
Content
In whom they were
And what they did.

It was
That a great yearning
Filled him
And he did not
Fit in
With the bustle
Of the other.

Winchester saw
The opening

To eternity
And he wanted
To dwell there.

He had a mere taste
And wanted more.

To hunger for Truth
How
The substance
Of what is there
Summons
The drive of passion
Onto horizons
Beyond time and space.

It is
In the blood
Of the artist
That Shields designs
The moment
That pictures
The authentic article
And it is
Within the bounds
Of her destiny
To capture the look
In heart.

Following the flight
That the crows carve
In the sky
She leaps into becoming
As the rhythm
Of cosmic consciousness
Fills her with vision.

As images of becoming there
Light the way
Through a parabola
Of time
She seizes
The close at hand
And colors a two
Dimensional reality
With the blood
Of the always
Already there.

Then
Thoughts probe
Possibility
Revealing the way
The Truth and the life.

Mounted on her hog
Riding through
A wilderness of possibility
Hope felt the rush
From the living moment
Pull mind
Into the deep touch.

It was
A time when heart
Found self
In the mirror
Brewing the dynamic
That launched becoming there
Into pure magic.

Then
She stopped at the edge
Of time and space
Because mystery consumed
What was there.

Through her third eye
She beheld
The principalities
Governing the celestial clocks
And they moved her
Into a parabola of time.

There
She felt the war
Fought in heart.

Turning
To The Unknown Goede
She heard trumpets
Of the everlasting
And The Counselor
Equipped her
With the battlements
Of Truth.

Then
She remounted her hog
And headed to eternity.

In the darkness
A streetlight
Features a tree
Its leaves turning
To gold.

As autumn issued
Its change
His dream
Steadied his vision.

He saw a man
Hiding in a wilderness
As crows
Brought him manna
Each morning.

Those were times
When reality touched
Becoming there
With the spirit
Of cosmic consciousness
And faith conquered
The doubt cast
By the darkness.

So
A figure of change
Reinvented
Time and space
As Truth
Wrote upon the heart.

With this vision
Winchester looked
To the mystery tree
Finding a moment
Of meaning.

Then
A dawn
Of everlasting
Showered him
With a thirst
As he listened
To the song
Of becoming.

Meditating
On The Word
He encountered the breath
Of becoming there
And he felt the embrace
Of what mattered.

So
His dream took him
To the other side
Where an eternal light
Filled him
With secrets of being
And time.

So
Socrates taught
How to think
And Jesus of Nazareth taught
How to believe.

Mounted on her hog
Riding through
A wilderness of possibility
Hope felt the rush
From the living moment
Pull mind
Into the deep touch.

It was
A time when heart
Found self
In the minute particular
Brewing the dynamic
That launched becoming there
Into pure magic.

Then
She stopped
At the edge
Of time and space
Because mystery consumed
What was there.

Through her third eye
She beheld
The principalities
In the celestial clocks

And they moved her look
Into a parabola of time.

There
She felt the war
Fought in heart.

Turning
To The Unknown God
She heard the trumpets
Of the everlasting
And The Counselor
Equipped her
With the battlements
Of Truth.

Then
She remounted her hog
And headed to eternity.

In the darkness
Only the close
At hand stiurs mind
Because the horizon
Hides in the pitch.

In the shadows
All there is

Are the lamps
From the garden
Of tables and chairs.

So
A café in the darkness
Becomes home
For the wandering
As the artists
Gather their spirits
And the starry night
Showers time
With epiphany.

It was
An age when the night
Told the bones
Of eternity
A certain Truth
While images explored
Time and space
And the artist lit
Becoming there
With the authentic
Article.

Then
Vashakmadze entered
The forsaken forest
That was struck

With fire
And shades of grey
Pronounced desolation.

In their charred bodies
The trees spoke
Of death
Yet life resurrected
Was their destiny.

So
There was beauty
In life
And a certain beauty
In death
Because Truth endures
Forevermore.

So
Hope rose in the night
Of swirling orbs
As the deep touch
Led her
Into a stirring
Of magic.

There was
The ebb of becoming there

And the flow
Of thought
In the darkness
When she found
A portal
To the other side.

Although time ceased
She seized
That moment
And found
Truth
Among the debris
Of another reality.

How
Mind ventures
Beyond the heart beat
Of the now
And into the wilderness
Of possibility
And how it
Seeks the bed rock
Of what matters.

Then
Hope soars
Into a starry night
Taken into the folds
Of cosmic consciousness

While the earth dangles
In mystery.

How
The world spins
In nothingness
As the power
Of The Unknown God
Defines the physics
Of time and space.

So
Mind departs
The dull round
As Hope reaches
Into pockets
Of enlightenment
And she grasps
What is there.

How
Truth is found
In the bones
Of eternity.

When there is
Possibility
There is always
Hope.

So
Heart is the passion
That drives mind
And mind serves
The heart
With reason.

On the other side
Of the abyss
Dwells cosmic consciousness
Sending emanations
Through time and space
Spiriting thought
Into the close at hand.

It is there
Where a vertical column
Of time
Establishes eternity
Governed
By The Unknown God.

It is there
Where predestination
Lives in the heart
Of The Word

A place
Beyond the linear.

It is there
Where Hope looks
For images of Truth
As the artist
In her
Reaches through
Her third eye.

Climbing
Out of her self
Hope finds the deep touch
Penetrating
The substance of being
And time.

As a parabola of time
Connects her
To the beyond
She feels The Counselor
Move her trance
Into the authentic article.

Then
Winchester, her muse
Takes her
Into the living moment
And the muscle

Of becoming there
Secures her faith
Into the will
To be.

In the garden
Of tables and chairs
Hope sketched
An old man
In tones of blue
Drinking his morning
Coffee.

Humble
Before the day
He seemed dedicated
To life
And the freedoms
In life.

Believing himself
Into becoming there
He carried his faith
In visions
Of what could
Have been
And Hope took

To the signs
Of his age.

Then
Trumpets sounded
And angels
Carried him away.

There was
The inkling of a miracle
In the air
As she drew the moment
With reverent thought.

How
Times and a half
Close the moment
Sealing it
With treasures
Of memories
True in spirit.

So
In life there are
Always sweet memories
As time connects
To form and substance.

To save
The moment
Of transformation
How
The spirit encompasses
Becoming there
As life
Onto forevermore
Sounds
Before a cup of coffee.

So
The old man leaves
With the spirit of Truth
In his last breath.

So
A principality visited
Hope with an agenda.

It spoke
With thoughts
Of authority
Ruling the moment.

It knew
The coming and going
Of linear time

And controlled
What was there.

There was
A car barreling
Down the road
In oncoming traffic
And it did not
Stop at the sign.

The principality
Commanded Hope
To swerve
Into his lane
And she did.

Rage
In the driver
Of the oncoming car
Exploded.

There was a gun.

Then
It was over.

It all seemed
A lesson
Teaching that there are
Powers

Beyond the here
And now
That have a play
In phenomenal reality.

So
Was the incident
Worth dying for
But the principality
Had control
Of the moment.

How
Fragile the thread
Of life
Where destiny hangs.

So
From the unknown
Come signals and signs
And the crows
Carry messages
From the beyond.

To understand
What is there
Takes a reading
Between phenomenal

Realities
As Hope eases
Into trance.

Once there
The moons of Truth
Shine
Upon thought
And time opens
Possibility
As beauty rises
From the earth.

Then
Becoming there
Among the throws
Of cosmic consciousness
Summons
The bones of Truth
To stand
Among the living.

How
The mystery
Of end times
Echoes
Through the spaces
Of mind
And thoughts stagger

Under the weight
Of eternity.

Then
Hope turns
To The Unknown God
And the glory
Of faith fills her
With the breath
Of life.

How
Beautiful the angels
Sing
As times and a half
Open to blessings.

Then
Hope embraces
Her muse
With the passion
Of the everlasting
As they grow
Into the eternal beauty
Of Truth.

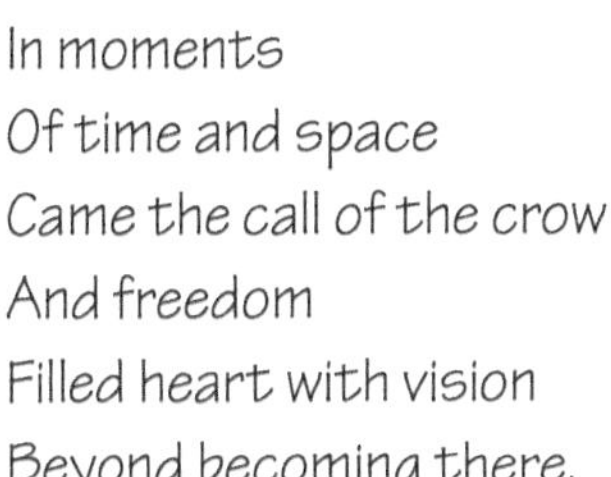

In moments
Of time and space
Came the call of the crow
And freedom
Filled heart with vision
Beyond becoming there.

On the other side
Of time and space
Hope gathered the look
Of the given
As the unknown
Materialized
In mind.

It was
The reach into possibility
That brought breath
To self
As the tongue
Of the everlasting
Whispered Truth
Into a valley
Of dried bones.

How
The life of freedom
Flourishes
When mind connects

To the mystery
Of being and nothingness.

Then
Hope channels
The deep touch
While the crow seats
In the center
Of what matters.

Then
The song of liberty
Emerges from silence.

So
Truth begins and prospers
In the blood of freedom.

SECTION 3

Within the Other

So
There are three
Dimensions to time::
A vertical column of time
A parabola of time
And linear time.

So
There are three types
Of time keepers:
The cosmic clock
The celestial clocks
And the biological clock.

A vertical column of time
Is kept
By the cosmic clock
And is the province
Of omnipresence.

It is the source
Of all and everything.

It is the posture
Of The Unknown God.

The parabola of time
Is kept
By the celestial clocks

And is the province
Of principalities.

Here is
The mechanism of destiny.

It is the trace between
The cosmic clock
And the biological clock.

It is
Present as a suspension
Of time
In the sense of the moment.

Linear time
Is kept
By the biological clock
And measures
Phenomenal reality.

It is
The domain of self
And the close at hand.

Traditional art
Liberates becoming there
Through the deep touch
While virtual art
Captures phenomenal reality

Through the magic
Of the mirror.

To live
Moment by moment
Is to sense Truth
Through the third eye.

So
Angels encompassed
Shield's mind
As the duduk
Spread mystery
Behind a nation's
Pain.

How
Her heart groaned
Upon hearing the lament
Of a people's cry
For deliverance.

Then
They gathered
In a great room
And Vashakmadze
Displayed ideation
In soft blue tones.

It was
The movement
Of misery
Through the blood
Of becoming there
As substance
Overflowed the skull
Of what mattered.

There
In the form
Of desolation
The earth cried out
And cosmic consciousness
Measured the magnitude
Of suffering.

Then
Hope's muse
Covered his eyes
With smoke and fire
As time wore thin
And the breath
Of the given
Yielded
The deep touch
To flesh and bone.

How
The somber tones
Of life lost
In pain
Embedded into
A music
Of always and forever.

So
The picture
Of a land of beauty
Unfolded Truth
To the believers.

It is that
The artist
Must endure
The dull round
With its callous ways
As poverty
Is but one
Of the challenges
An artist must endure.

To be
A messenger
Of Truth

How
The heart gently weeps
But there are no
Ears to listen.

Then
The muse comes
To the moment
With a voice
Of comfort
Healing the wounds
From times
Again and again
Of suffering.

So
The artist learns
Humility
In the face
Of rejection
As the lesson
Pounded
Through time past
Bleeds life.

Although
Crippled by the day
By day
The artist rises
To the Truth

Holding fast
To the awesome work
Of The Unknown God.

Then
While listening
To the cry
Of the duduk
The artist
Gains strength
Knowing
That Truth conquers
The hollow
In becoming there.

So
Some day
The dull round
Will awaken.

So
Hope triumphs
Over the waste land
As The Word
Infuses
A right spirit.

To Winchester
His dream
Moved in mysterious ways
With the magic
Behind the here and now
As her pleasure.

She adorned herself
With the radiance
Of possibility
As her blue eyes
Penetrated
Time and space.

For Winchester
His dream
Was the opiate
That infused him
With want
Until he could taste
Her living moment.

How
He heaved
In the throws
Of his want
As her third eye
Carried him
Into total rapture.

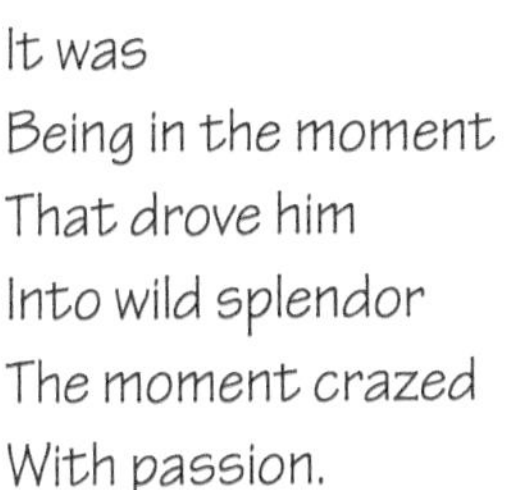

It was
Being in the moment
That drove him
Into wild splendor
The moment crazed
With passion.

Then
He saw
Her third eye
As a portal
To the other side
As his blood
Turned
To liquid fire.

She
Inspired him to climb
Out of himself
And engage the unknown.

She seduced him
With her deep touch
And he yielded
His throat
For the kill.

In her grip
He found Truth

And the power
Of cosmic consciousness.

To escape
From the confines
Of evil
The artist receives the power
Resident in Truth
And freedom unlocks
Mind.

How
Pain has taught
The artist
Unrelenting suffering
And the deceit
Of the dull round.

In an inferno
Of hate
Life is consumed
As Hope clings
To her faith
For deliverance.

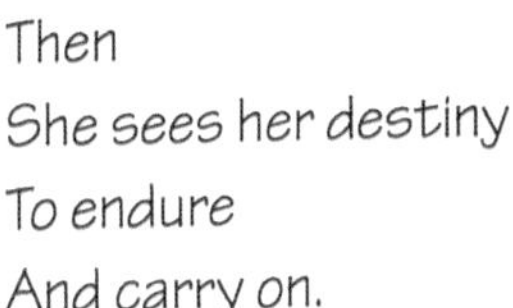

Then
She sees her destiny
To endure
And carry on.

Although
Crippled by injustice
She forms the beauty
Of the everlasting
Lifting her third eye
Into the heavens.

Married to Truth
She climbs
Out of the pit
Her strength powered
By the deep touch.

With the freedom
Of faith
Cosmic consciousness
Infuses visions
Of Truth
In an age
Of disinformation.

It was
In the mountains
Of Tennessee
That he returned
To the moment
When he met
His dream.

She was his dwelling place.

Through the connection
To her third eye
Winchester found
The portal
To the other side
Where the authentic
Article
Fed moments
Of passion.

As he engaged
A parabola of time
Linear reality
Dissolved
And the celestial clocks
Took him
Into beauty and Truth.

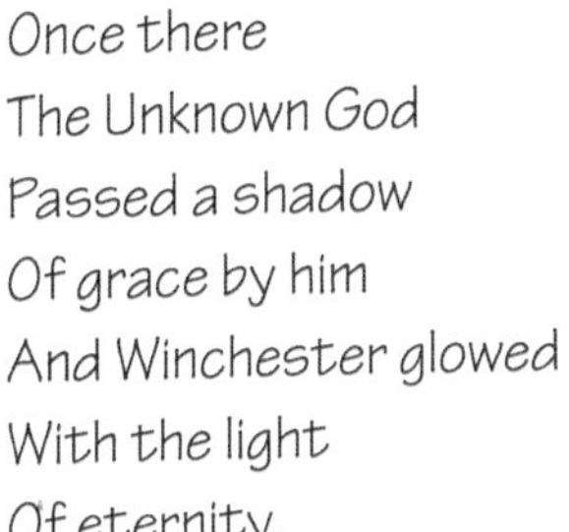

Once there
The Unknown God
Passed a shadow
Of grace by him
And Winchester glowed
With the light
Of eternity.

Then
His dream took
Hold of him
As together
They rode
Into the wilderness
Their hog
Penetrating time
And space.

So
It was true love
That owned into him
And the mountains
Spoke treasures
Into heart and mind.

How
The anthem
Of freedom filled time
And times and a half
As they followed

The call of eternity
And The Unknown God
Blessed their travels.

Together
They explored the unknown.

How
The moment of Truth
Opens becoming there
To a trance
Taking Shields
Beyond time and space
As she peals off
Self-deception.

She
Liberated from the jaws
Of the linear
Travels into the unknown
Seized by an epiphany
As her deliverance
Gives her visions
Of the everlasting.

Although
The dull round tries
To bury her

In disinformation
She believes herself
Into being
Beyond its reach.

By tying herself
To freedom. Mind
Accelerates
Through nothingness
As her substance
Breathes in life.

There is
The deep touch
In her configuration
Enduring
Onto forevermore
As masks dance
Into a horizon
Of blood.

Beyond time, beyond space
Beyond becoming there
Shields inhales
Cosmic consciousness
And what matters most
Takes her form
Into ecstasy.

Although
Living in an era
Of darkness
She holds Truth
As her destiny.

Digging deep
Into the unknown
The artist connects
To cosmic consciousness
And the muse
Beholds light in darkness.

Although
Shields draws Truth
Into becoming there
The dull round
Blind to what matters
Writhes in madness.

There is
A wilderness of thought
In the message
On the cave wall
As images celebrate
The deep touch
And mind advances
Beyond nothingness.

Then
Shields takes
To the wind
Soaring into the liberation
Of time and space
And the masks
Of deception rot
In the4 hollows
Of the moment.

How
True the echo
Of eternity in the heart
Of becoming there
As Shields configures
Destindestin.

Then
The Unknown God
Showers her
With the peace
Beyond understanding
As her third eye
Accepts a connection
To a vertical
Column of time.

So
Becoming there finds
Home
In the garden
Of tables and chairs.

It is
A place where thought
Opens treasures
From the beyond
As mind probes
The unknown
To reveal the heart
Of what matters.

Although
At the edge
Of nothingness
The artist stirs the mystery
Of the everlasting
And the deep touch
Spirits the other
Into the authentic
Article.

Then
The cry of the duduk
Took becoming there
Across times and a half
As possibility

Sets milestones
In what is there.

All at once
A trumpet sounded
And the tears
Of ages past
Found joy
In the given.

To transform
The abyss
Into the gift
Of the covenant
How
The artist traces
The face of Truth
Into being and time.

In the darkness
Time and space
Are one
As the magic
Of becoming there
Turns
Into the deep touch.

Then
Hope presents
The image
Of a silhouette
Dancing
To the rhythm
Of the celestial clocks
As the drums
Of eternity
Open the moment
To cosmic consciousness.

There is
The echo of what
Matters
Leading to an epiphany
As the senses
Eclipse
Hidden meaning.

So
Hope focuses
On the way
To the other side
Of being and time
When she connects
To her muse
And Winchester equips her
With the third eye.

So
She works the image
Of thought
Beyond mind
As she listens
To a song of sorrow.

How
The duduk pulls
The heart into tears.

How
From pain Truth comes.

So
The image
Of an old man's tears
Frames
The form and substance
Of the dance.

How
The message
Of Truth
Becomes the miracle
Of life.

So
He awakens
An epiphany
As the splendor
Of the sunrise issues
Hope
In The Word.

So
The sunrise belongs
To the form
Of Truth
And the beauty
Of it all
Spells mystery
Into the bones
Of becoming there.

Then
Hope mounted her hog
And headed east
Into the wilderness
And her muse
Followed her.

Passing
From one horizon
To another
They sought the origin
Of what matters

As The Unknown God
Displayed
The grandeur
Of the moment.

There is
The deep touch
In the rolling thunder
That echoes
Through times and a half
While they connected
To cosmic consciousness
While they rode
Destiny
Into the miracle
Of life.

How
The magic
Carried by the wind
Transfigures
What is there
Into a two-dimensional
Reality
As they climbed
Out of themselves
Into the liberty
Of the land.

To be free
In the harvest
Of spirit
How
Hope masters
The ride to eternity.

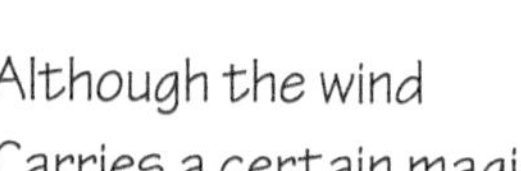

Although the wind
Carries a certain magic
The artist depicts
Mountains unburdened
By the turbulence.

They have
A magic all their own.

With a low sky
Rubbing the horizon
Time becomes a moment
As the rain pours
Treasure into mind.

Looking off
To a wilderness valley
The artist seizes
The grandeur

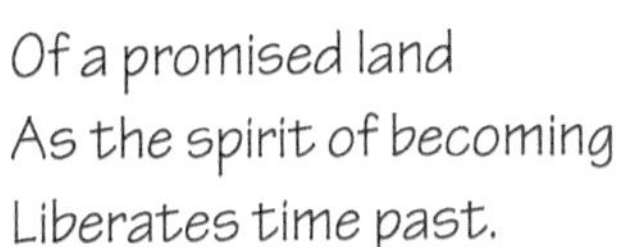

Of a promised land
As the spirit of becoming
Liberates time past.

Then
Marching from the immediate
A squad of old soldiers
Advances
Their eyes hollow
With the horror
They have seen
And the artist follows them
As the cry of the duduk
Speaks of sacrifice.

To be
At the very edge
Of gore
And yet endure
How
War digs a pit
Of vile memories.

Then
A dove lands
In the garden
Of tables and chairs.

Because
There is art in life
The artist lives Truth
    - Or so Shields believes
As decades pass.

It is
A wondrous passion
A destiny, a calling
That reaches into the heart
Of becoming there.

As the blood
Of an artist's life
Art nourishes the other
Reaching Truth.

So
Shields listened
To the song of eternity
Seeing the place
Of being and time
As she advanced
Beyond the reaches
Of time future.

All the while
In the garden
Of tables and chairs
Shields listened

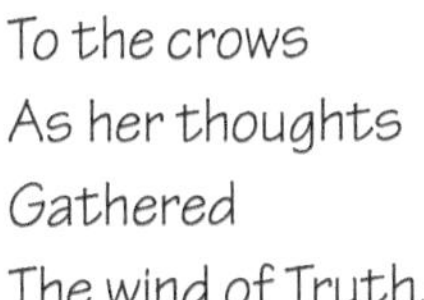

To the crows
As her thoughts
Gathered
The wind of Truth.

When she opened
Her third eye
The rush of passion
Launched visions
As thoughts poured
From a portal
In cosmic consciousness.

To see beauty
In tears of sorrow
She looked
Into the eyes of van Gogh
Finding Truth
As her destiny.

How
The darkness
Of the other side
Connects becoming there
To nothingness
As the substance
Of what matters

Traverses
Down the road
To the actual.

Throttling
With the blood
Of the always already
There
Hope stretches
The linear
Into a parabola
Of time.

Then
The wilderness speaks
A language
Of tongues
To the heart
And her muse
Tightens his grip
Upon the milestones
To the beyond.

He is
Her anchor
Bringing her back
From the unknown.

Although Hope
Traverses being
And nothingness
She turns
To her muse
And he follows
Her trace to Truth.

So
It is in her painting
That the unknown
Surfaces
As the deep touch
Connects
To the essence
Of times and a half.

So
The magic
Of the road
Fills her with images
That carry mind
Into the drift
Of things in themselves.

How
The colors
Of eternity
In her eyes

Form a view
Of the splendor
In the moment.

Cruising
Through time and space
Hope uncovered
The mystery
Within becoming there
As the hymn
Of forevermore
Saturated the moment.

It was
A tribute
To the power
Of The Unknown God
That she found
Blessed assurance
And the road
Glistened
With promise.

To be
Delivered from fields
Of blood
And taste

The freedom
In the wind
How
Fortunate she felt
In leaving
The catacombs
Of desperation.

There were
Times when the dull round
Ground her meat
Into dust
But she clung
To the promise
Of The Word
The rock
Of her faith.

Winchester, her muse
Through all of it
Remained faithfully
At her side
Even in the darkest
Of moments.

So
She survived
The horror

Of war
And being surrounded
With suffering and death.

How
The wounds
Of the past
Left echoes
In mind
But they faded
When she rode
Through the wilderness
With the authentic article
In her heart.

Across the way
A hawk perched
On a limb
Surrounded by the spirits
Of the wilderness
As the third eye
Brought Hope
Into a taste of need.

Wondering what mattered
To the substance of the other
She needed to know

Where her journey
Was taking her
As the now
Clouded her connection
To cosmic consciousness.

Although thought plots
The course of mind
The heart looks
To the hawk
For the way of a warrior
And Hope steps
Inside a moment.

As her trance
Carries time and space
Into a two
Dimensional reality
She feels the eclipse
Of need
And the deep touch
Takes mind
Beyond the now.

Then
The hawk stirs
Taking flight
Into the unknown
And hope leaves need
To follow Truth.

So
Need is blind
To destiny and captive
Of the immediate now
As the spirits
Of the wilderness
Bring vision
To the moment.

So
A warrior has
No need to know
Because living in the moment
Is destiny.

Crowding
The garden
Of tables and chairs
A fleet of angels sang
To the blue of eternity
And a gypsy princes
Adorned the moment
With her immaculate beauty.

Patches of clouds
Allowed the blue
To bring Vashakmadze

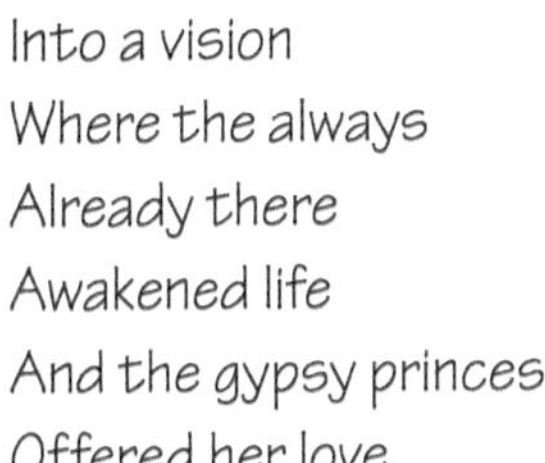

Into a vision
Where the always
Already there
Awakened life
And the gypsy princes
Offered her love.

It was
The hymn to praise
The Unknown God
That brought promise
To the land
As tulips and daffodils
Flourished.

Then
The angels took
Vashakmadze
And his gypsy princes
To the other side
Of being and nothingness.

Then
Truth filled the moment.

As the celestial clocks
Summoned destiny
The wind whispered
The given
Into becoming there

And Vashakmadze
A young artist
Portrayed his love.

Then
The angels smiled.

So
Hope chased
The wind
With her hog
Growling
Through the frontier
Of mind.

Stopping
At the side
Of the Tennessee River
She sat
Sketching the substance
Of what was there.

It was
A scene of the deep
Wilds
Resonating

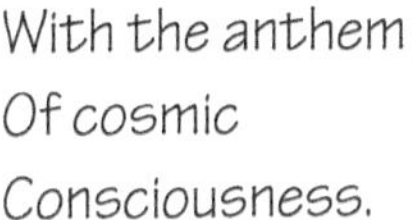

With the anthem
Of cosmic
Consciousness.

Touching the beyond
Hope drew
The hidden meaning
In phenomenal reality
Because
The close at hand
Is there
As a touch stone
To Truth.

Then
An image
Of wonder
Graced the moment
As form follows
Substance
And the unknown
Presented shadows
Of thought.

As Hope pursued
Her trance
She listened
To the rhythm of drums

Pounding life
Into the liberty
Of the given.

Then
The sun exploded
Through the drift
Of clouds
As Hope depicted
The other side
Of being and time.

So
To behold Truth
Hope opened
Her third eye
And the awesome
Power
Of The Unknown God
Moved shadows
Into light.

Riding the road
To eternity
In a rush of wind
Hope moved
Into a two dimensional

Reality
And linear time
Dissolved
Into a moment.

It was
A type of trance
As body and machine
Became one
And mind scaled
The walls
Of oblivion.

There
Upon the road
The deep touch
Reached her
And memories
Of being
With Winchester
Rose
Into the here and now.

It was
A moment
When time present
Took mind
To an arousal
Of becoming there.

Then
She groaned.

Opening her third eye
Hope
Filled with the heat
Of passion
And memory constituted
The span
Of what mattered.

So
Truth knows
True love
As Winchester
Embraced
Her substance
As desire flooded
Her form.

There was
Life in the moment
That traversed
The possible
Through the magic
Of true love.

So
True love is
A reality of its own.

Then
The fog was thick
And Hope navigated
Slowly
Because the road
Disappeared.

At best
There was little
Visibility
On the mountain ridge
But she rode
With Winchester
To help find
The way.

With a prayer
On their lips
They asked The Word
To show the way.

Then
In the distance
They saw the lights
Of the garden
Of tables and chairs
As they eased
Through nothingness.

So
The reality in fog
Is so much different
Than times of clarity.

It was that
There was no
Close at hand.

All there was
Was a light
In the distance.

To travel
Through phenomenal
Reality
When blindness
Defines the moment.

How
Becoming there loses self
While in the hands
Of the abyss.

So
They placed
Their trust
In the way
The Truth and the life.

So
Shields filled
Winchester's dreams
That night
With the sweat of love.

There was
The embrace
Of wild passion that throbbed
Through his body
As the little death
Encompassed
His sleep
Over and over again.

From the interstices
Of mind
A fire blazed
Caused by the rub
Of the deep touch
And Winchester heaved
Breathless want
Beneath the stars.

Spreading heat
Across the moment
She piled her form

Upon his time
And they glowed
With ecstasy.

Then
She pulled him
Into her third eye
As the masks
Of hidden meaning
Danced
Into the unknown
And heart felt
The rush
Of their awesome sex.

It was
A dream lit sleep
That took him
Into the beyond
As the moment
Of pure bliss enveloped
Becoming there.

While
Cosmic consciousness
Fed the substance
Of their life
With Truth
They viewed

The celestial clocks
Gathering the energy
To be.

So
In the twilight
Of what mattered
Shields dissolved magic
In his dreams
And he placed Truth
In her space.

While this rain came
The mockingbird
Did not sing
And the crow did not fly.

It was
A steady rain
And becoming there reached
Into cosmic consciousness
Seeking
The rise of Truth
Into time present.

Although there was
A chill, a dreary dampness
To the wind

That sunk into bone
Hope painted
The grey of the sky
And the yellow
Of the daffodils
With the passion
Of the deep touch.

Then
Time and space
Triggered thought
As images
Of the close at hand
Led
To the awakening
Of the other.

Looking through the mirror
Of phenomenal reality
Hope found a trace
To Truth
As the possibility
Opened the unknown
And she built
A message
In a parabola of time
Depicting a lush valley
Of daffodils.

How
Heart filled
With the power of life
As her message
Defined the dimensions
Of self and the other.

When the rain
Eased up
A mocking bird
Advanced eternity's entrance
In the stretch of the moment.

So
There was
A still life
A silver decanter
The central pointy
And the shadows
And highlights
Brought Hope
Into what matters.

Vashakmadze
A young master
Worked his way
Through being

And time
Giving breath
To the still life.

It is
The apprehension

Of the thing
In itself
Projected
From the other side
That brings Truth
To the mind
As heart loads
With the authentic
Article.

Then
Hope leaped
Into the moment
Finding the magic
Of what matters.

How
A two-dimensional
Reality
Suspends times
And a half
As the message

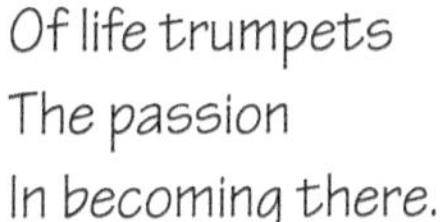

Of life trumpets
The passion
In becoming there.

There was
A revelation
Of the minute
Particular
As the colors
Spoke a rhythm
Of wonder.

Although
The way through
The beyond
Is unknown
Vashakmadze
Presented the image
Of beauty
In possibility.

So
The still life
By Vashakmadze
Brought the breath
Of angels into Hope.

When thoughts are
Sparse
And the heavy hand
Of the dull round
Makes becoming there
A stretch
Hope turns
To The Unknown God
As her muse
Mirrors eternity.

So
Pulling from possibility
She looks
To the rhythm
Of cosmic
Consciousness
And the movement
Of angels.

There
In the clouds
Of the everlasting
An idea forms
And the substance
Of what matters
Drops into mind.

Then
Hope embraces
Her muse
As the colors
Of always and forever
Flood
The ends
Of ideation.

How
The purple mountain
Majesty
Tells the heart
Of the muscle
Of Truth
As mind pierces
Hidden meaning
As a moment
Is born.

Then
Her muse takes her
To the treasures
Of the beyond
As the will
In the blood
Uncovers
The beauty of forevermore.

So
The moment
Explodes
With wonder.

While in the garden
Of tables and chairs
Hope and van Gogh
Discussed
How art revealed
Truth
And how the artist
A messenger of the beyond
Connected
To cosmic consciousness
Through the deep touch.

Then
The crows spoke
To heart
As a hawk sharpened
Mind
And the muse
Of the ages unraveled
Being and time.

It was
That becoming there surfaced
Through the gift
From the given
That what mattered most
Looked
Through the third eye
Feeding substance
To life.

It was
That substance
Preceded form
While form wrote Truth
In the light shed
Upon the close at hand.

Suspending time
Into a moment
The artist allowed
The other
To view the sounds
Carried by the wind.

How
Speaking images
In the moment
Brought the other
Hope.

Then
The song of eternity
Lifted becoming there
Into trumpets
Of time and space
And the artist
Sketched a vision
Of a starry night
Reaching into the always
Already there.

To be born
Into the given
Allowed life to receive
The promise of forevermore.

Hope understood
And so did van Gogh.

While in trance
Hope
Surveyed phenomenal
Reality
Through her third eye
As mind danced
To the drums
Of hidden meaning.

It was
Her way to the other
Side
Where Truth
Emanated messages
Of the authentic
Article.

Then
Images presented
Things
In themselves
And her muse
Embraced the moment
With passion.

How
Her third eye
Revealed
The mystery
Of The Unknown God
As time and space
Were one
In a vertical column
Of time.

So
Hope drew
The message
Of being toward

Nothingness
When the substance
Of the unknown
Massaged mind
Until Truth surfaced.

There is
A connection
Where being faces
Nothingness.

There is
A connection
Between Hope
And Winchester
That feeds becoming there.

How
Passion drives the moment.

How all things are
Possible
Through the deep touch
Of The Word.

Then
It is winter
In Tennessee

And a slow rain
Drizzles.

The weather
Brings out the ache
In the bones.

An old man
Smokes his pipe
As the darkness
Before dawn
Covers
What is there
But
In the garden
Of tables and chairs
There is light
Acknowledging
The arrival
Of tomorrow.

Memories
Of times and a half
Color
The way he looks
His grey hair
Combed
By the wind.

Then
Vashakmadze shares
A painting with him
A portrait
Of who he had
Become.

He never thought
Of being
An old man
But one day he awoke
And the mirror
Told the Truth.

Vashakmadze's painting
Was another mirror.

The old man
Passed some words
As he puffed
On his pipe
As he drank
His morning coffee.

How
Old age is not
Just a number
But the proof
Of endurance.

How
He had always
Considered himself
A survivor.

As the clouds
Drift
Over the mountains
Hope Shields
Pursues cosmic
Consciousness
Through her trance.

Pulling
On times and a half
She emerges
Into the unknown
Where the moment
Forms
A slice of Truth.

It is
A landscape
Of golden grandeur
As the trees
Display their bones.

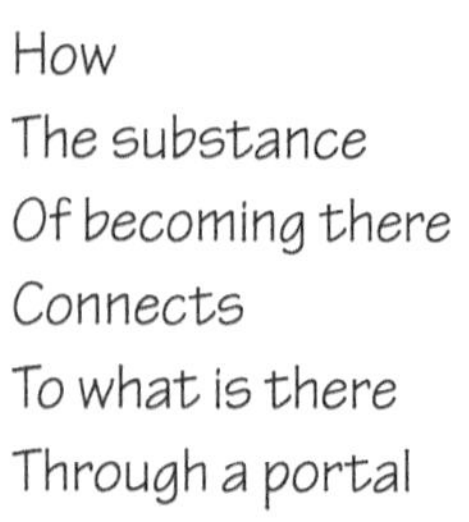

How
The substance
Of becoming there
Connects
To what is there
Through a portal
To the beyond.

Presenting
A two-dimensional reality
She suspends
The look
Of what matters
As being and nothingness
Feel
The third eye.

Blind
To the dull round
She takes
To the other side
Where beauty
Dances
As her muse
Feeds her
With wild passion.

There is
An undressing
Of hidden meaning

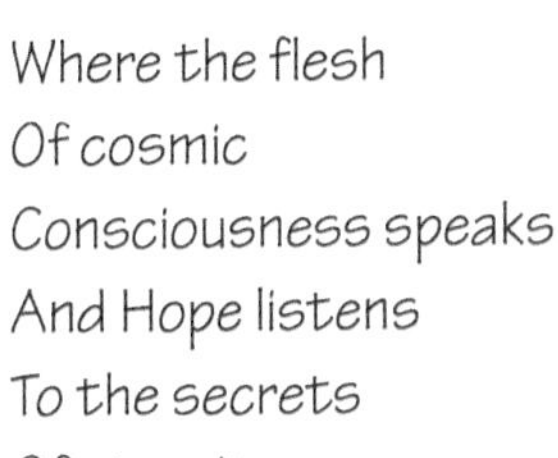

Where the flesh
Of cosmic
Consciousness speaks
And Hope listens
To the secrets
Of eternity.

So
The colors of destiny
Bleed
Into the arousal
Of Truth.

Unearthing
The architecture
Of time and space
Hope felt
The physics
Of the authentic
Article
As cosmic consciousness
Endowed becoming there
With a vision
Beyond understanding.

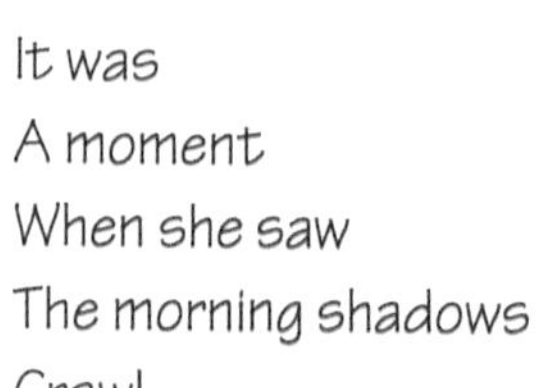

It was
A moment
When she saw
The morning shadows
Crawl.

Then
She drifted
Across her canvas
As an image
Appeared in mind.

Two figures
Took hold
Of what was there
And two rings
Of gold
Eclipsed the setting.

It was
A matter of substance
Infusing form
With mystery
As figure and ground
Displaced
Phenomenal reality
And the deep touch
Moved Hope
Toward The Unknown God.

How
The artist reveals
The hidden meaning
In the unknown
As eons bury
The moment
In flesh and blood.

Probing the abyss
She seized
The vibration
Of colors
That transformed
Being from nothingness.

How
The idea passed
Passion
Into a moment
When The Word
Gave the artist in her
A whole world
Of Truth.

He was
A memory that surfaced
From time to time

And Hope knew
Of his passion.

How
Truth was the rudiment
Of his life
As he grew
Into a testament
Of becoming there.

So
He became her muse
A face
Hungering in her
Shadows
As her thoughts
Surveyed possibility.

He was there
As she probed
The unknown
And he
Opened the way
To the beyond.

Then
One day he was
A song

Calling her
As he pulled images
Of wonder into mind.

She answered
Her muse
With visions
Of everlasting
As he became
A portal
To the deep touch.

How
The connection
To her muse
Surpassed understanding
And they breathed
Together
The same breath
In the depths
Of life.

Together
They filled form
With the substance
Of what mattered
And their devotion
To cosmic consciousness
Became the signature
Of their bond.

As the traffic
Drives into destiny
His dream
Launches thoughts
And images
Of thoughts.

His mind
Sees them
As soldiers
Dedicated to one
Cause
To serve and protect freedom.

Armed
With the weapons
Of Truth
They roil across
Time and space
With thunder
In their muscle
As they spit fire
Into the wind.

So
The oppressors
Have infiltrated

The land
Of the free and brave
But the drums
Of destiny
Hunt them down.

It is
The rhythm
Of the celestial clocks
That overshadows
The moment
As each soldier readies
For battle
Against tyranny.

How
Their fists pound
Power
Into the heart
Of becoming there
As the traffic
Carries the banner
Of Truth.

There is
An anthem
Sung
Into their blood
That gives them

Courage
As the war
Against tyranny
Turns
To Armageddon.

So
It is the war
To end all wars.

Looking
Into the waters
Of the Tennessee River
Winchester slips
Into seeing
The flight of destiny
As a life
Breathes in
The everlasting.

So
Mind registers
A moment
When crows tell
The tale
Of forevermore
And Winchester calls

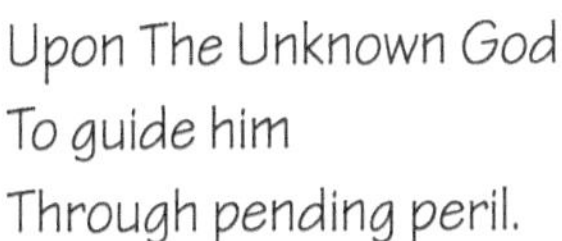

Upon The Unknown God
To guide him
Through pending peril.

It is
By faith that he
Rides through time
And space
Headed for the beyond
And his dream
Fills him
With her passion.

It is
Perhaps his purpose
To witness
The coming of the kingdom
Of glory
And his dream gives him
The elixir
Of being and time
To clear his mind.

How
The vision gathered
By the reflection
Of the waters
Projects the substance
Of what is there

Into a treasure
As he gains
A life worth living.

It was
The grip of nothingness
That his dream
Severed
As Truth brought hope.

She
Configures his destiny
As an epiphany
Where The Word
Triumphs over all
According
To the cosmic clock.

At the edge
Of time and space
A siren whines
And tragedy knows
The last breath
In the darkness.

So
A body waits for a return
To the living

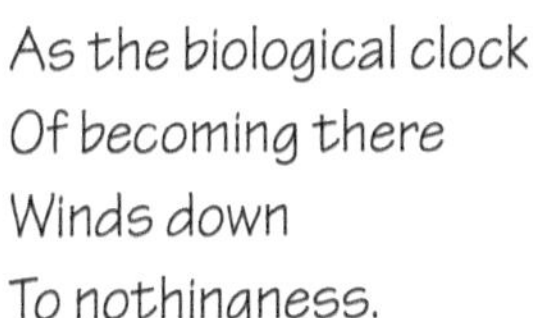

As the biological clock
Of becoming there
Winds down
To nothingness.

Heart attack.

How
Fragile this thing
Called life.

Then
The siren stops
And the darkness
Begs to cry out
For deliverance.

Silence.

Then
An old man
Searches the stars
For a way through
The unknown
As the signals
Of the here and now
Echo
Through his bones.

Holding
His wife's cold hand
He measures
Sixty years of marriage
Before the no longer.

So
Sweet memories
Are all
That is left.

What treasure they hold.

So
Hope rode the road
Of passion
As she pursued
The substance
Of things
In themselves.

Through trance
She connected
To cosmic consciousness
As times
Translated into moments
Of the deep touch.

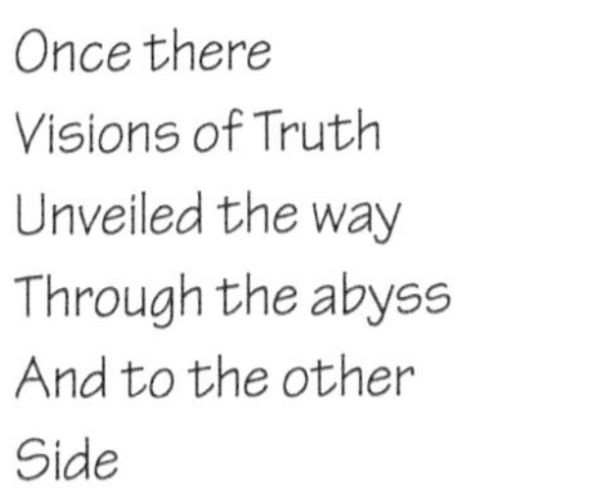

Once there
Visions of Truth
Unveiled the way
Through the abyss
And to the other
Side
Of being and nothingness.

Then
In a Roman coliseum
She pictured a crazed crowd
As a sword
Penetrated the heart
Of mankind.

There was
Blood on the ground
As the crowd
Drank in
The brutality
Of the moment.

How
White and shades
Of black
Colored the crowd
As the raised blade
And fist
Were the tone
Of the living.

Although the slayed
Was not shone
Death throws
Carried on and on.

How
The grandeur
Of The Unknown God
Delivers a message
Into the moment
As becoming there
Witnesses the power
Of the wilderness.

How
To grasp the splendor
Of the given
The deep touch penetrates
Mind
With the dagger
Of visions
Beyond time and space.

Looking into the expanse
From the top
Of Signal Mountain
Hope leaps

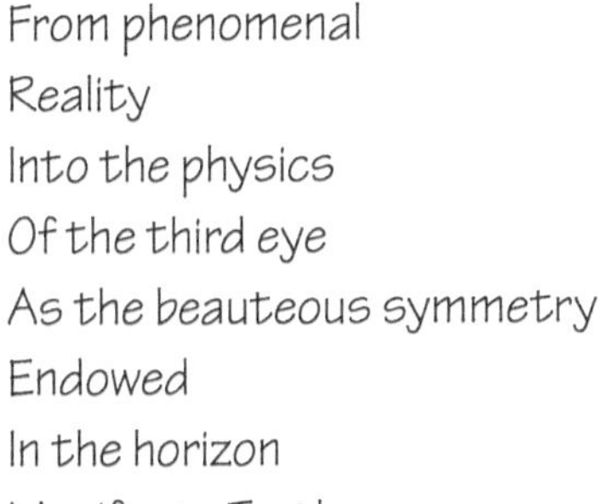

From phenomenal
Reality
Into the physics
Of the third eye
As the beauteous symmetry
Endowed
In the horizon
Manifests Truth.

Then
Hope circles
The message
From cosmic consciousness
And hidden meaning
Pounds life into becoming there.

It is
That the secrets
Of a vertical column
Of time
Offer the evidence
Of Truth
As the artist in Hope
Traces life
From the heart
Of what matters.

Then
They gathered
Together
Shields and Picasso
Vashakmadze and Dali
Grobowski and van Gogh.

They talked
About fauvism
And the radiant
Integration of colors
That gave life
To their gestures.

It was
That a two-dimensional
Reality
Was a step
Toward hidden meaning
Stirring the substance
Of what mattered.

It was
The articulation
Of the beyond
Into the form
Of the known
As the subject
Of the composition

Provided
The rhetoric of hidden
Meaning.

So
They laughed in moments
And growled in others
As the wits
Of masters probed
The rhythm
Of cosmic consciousness.

Although
The dull round
Could not grasp
The play
In their work
The masters trumpeted
With a singular voice
While becoming there
Took off
In a parabola of time.

So
In the garden
Of tables and chairs
They undressed
Phenomenal reality
To reveal the beauty
Of naked Truth.

So
There is always
Essence
Alive through cosmic
Consciousness
And it takes
Residence
In its existence
As the thing-in-itself.

From eternity
To eternity, self journeys
Through the unknown
As possibility sets
Before, during and after
The linearity
Of the biological clock.

Venturing
Into the dynamic
Of the celestial clocks
The mind
Penetrates a parabola
Of time
As the magic
Of what matters
Uncovers the existence

Of the always
Already there
As a touchstone.

Then
Winchester leaves
His biological clock
Climbing
Into a two-dimensional
Reality
Where he finds
The portal
To the deep touch.

There
His dream takes him
Into worlds beyond worlds
Where the living moment
Fulfills life
And she yields herself
To her passion.

So
The celestial clocks
Register destiny
In the silencer of the beyond
And the magic
Of Truth

Fills the persona
Of becoming there
With purpose.

How
Cognition
Of cosmic consciousness
Lifts outliving self
From becoming there
And The Unknown God
Gives breath to his destiny.

SECTION 4

A Portal to the Beyond

Although paralyzed
By the dull round
Hope struggled
To continue
With her muse
Onto the mystery
Of the given.

There was
The brutal fervor
Of times and a half
That opposed her efforts
In pursuing Truth.

Although there was
The climate
Of denial of the existence
Of Truth
Hope had the mission
To pronounce The Word
And the ways
Of The Word.

So
She meditated further
Where the substance
Of the beyond
Surfaced as visions.

Then
Mind warmed thoughts
To uncover images
As her brush
Illuminated
Time and space.

So
She fought
Against callous hearts
And she armed herself
With the power
Of The Deep Touch.

How
Pure the beauty
Of Truth.

How
True the message
Of forevermore.

So
Because there is
The Unknown God
There is Truth.

So
It was the crow
And the way of the crow
That taught
The connection
To cosmic consciousness
And Hope studied
The physics
Of the deep touch.

How
The voluntary functions
Work
In analogue iterations
While the involuntary system
Operates in digital

So
Mind is
The integration
Of these signals
From there to here.

As Hope meditated
The deep touch
Drew her
Into congruent patterns
Of what matters.

Then
Linear time and space
Of a three-dimensional
Reality
Triggers
The apprehension
Of phenomenal reality
As mind processes
The going
Of the here and now.

So
Hope registered
In a parabola
Of time
And a two-dimensional
Reality
To gather Truth.

How
The mechanism
Of becoming there
Found hidden meaning
In the crow
A teacher
From a wilderness
Of thought.

Her paintings are
The articulation of Truth.

So
It all points
To the chemistry
Of The Unknown God.

Deep in the center of mind
Cosmic consciousness
Connects thought
To a portal
In time and space
Through the third eye.

Above vultures circled
Hungry for death
To feed life
As drums pounded
The rhythm of substance
Into becoming there.

Then
Hope, taken by the wind
Of eternity
Liberated an image
A view
That expanded mind
Into the beyond.

So
The beginning of circles
Form time
Out of the blood
Of what matters.

Pushing ideation
Onto the edge
Of nothingness
Hope calculates
The dimensions
Of possibility
As Truth
Opens to the third eye.

It is
The birth of the moment
That triggers understanding
As the vultures
Find death
In the heart of the now.

Then
The drums spoke
Circles around death
As self found
The spirit of life
Within things in themselves.

How
Hope centered becoming there
Before a mirror
Finding the reflection
Of the unknown
While nothingness
Faded away.

So
The miracle of life
Trumps the magic of death.

So
Death is the beginning
Of the unknown.

The will to be
Pronounces the moment
When the artist
Depicts the majesty
Of the purple mountains.

Because
Hope eases the landscape
Into a vision
That surpasses thought
The other conquers

Self-deception
By grasping
The always already there.

It is
The message
Of the given
That defines becoming there
As the mountains
Testify to the mystery
Of life.

Probing the expanse
Hope offers the treasures
Found in hidden meaning
As the dignity
Of heart speaks Truth
Into the moment.

Then
Hope looked
To a graveyard
Where death began.

So
Death is not an end
But it is the beginning
Of the unknown.

Looking into the vast
Regions of the blue
Hope liberated the other
From the dull round
Because the landscape
Mirrored Truth.

She drew the image
Of the everlasting
And painted what mattered.

How
Becoming there is
A gift
From The Unknown God
As the mystery
Of the unending stepped
Into view.

So
The mystery and wonder
Of the substance
Of the close
At hand
Becomes grounded
By the cognition
Of the third eye.

In the connection
Between here and now
And cosmic consciousness
Rises a portal
Giving access to the beyond.

It is
That Truth surfaces
With meditation
Upon a two-dimensional
Reality
Where being and time
Become suspended
And moment
Affixes self
In the horizon
Of what is there
In the sounding
Of eternal drums.

Then
Visions stir
With the deep touch
And the drums
Of beyond feed
The passion
That drives the close
At hand
Into images of Truth.

To read
The messages
From the unknown
Mind eclipses
Phenomenal reality
And enters the ends
Of linear time and space.

Then
Clarity is born
From the mystery
And wonder
Of the here and now.

In a quiet rain
When becoming there
Reflects
Through a corridor
Of time
Mind reaches out
To touch
The authentic article.

How
Possibility intrudes
On the coming and going

Of linear time
With all and everything
On the horizon.

So
The Unknown God
And Truth
Belong to the possible
Although the immediate
Is blind
To what matters.

So
Each and every breath
Draws closer
To eternity
As the self
Clings
To the mask
Of self-deception

Then
Winchester turns
To his dream
And her smile
Opens
Time and times
And a half.

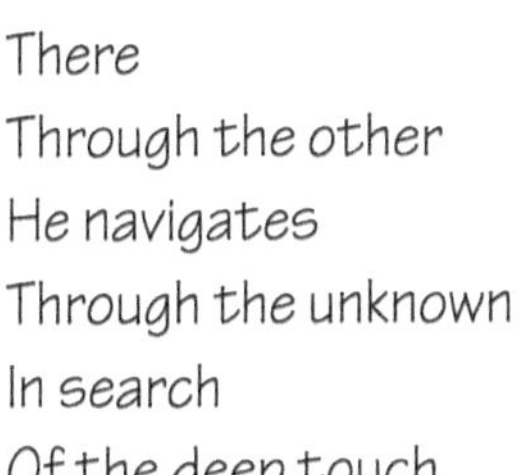

There
Through the other
He navigates
Through the unknown
In search
Of the deep touch.

How
faith requires a leap
from the given
because the always
already there defines
the mathematics
of being and time

Through the breath
of his biological clock
a vision appears
undressing
what is there
and his dream
takes mind
into the light
of the authentic article.

There
He sees Truth
And he places
His trust
In The Unknown God.

In the distance
A train rumbles
Headed for the unknown
And Winchester follows
The flight
Of a vulture
Shadowing
The here and now.

How necessity drives
Hunger
Into what is there
As life occupies
The immediate.

So
Winchester gathers
Visions
Of the beyond
As the minute particular
Yields its secrets.

To be
In a moment
When linear time
Dissolves
Into a two-dimensional
Reality

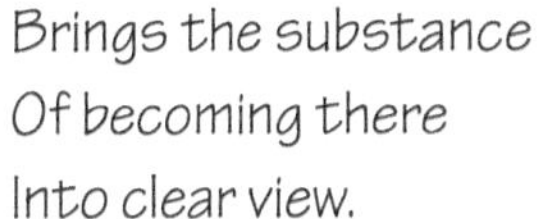

Brings the substance
Of becoming there
Into clear view.

Then
The wilderness
Of the expanse
Speaks magic, as eternity
Lights the movement
Of the deep touch
Into the heart.

How
Time bleeds Truth
Into mind
As faith governs
The travels
Of being in nothingness.

So
The Unknown God
Allows will
To be free
In linear time
But
In a vertical column
Of time
All is determined
And fixed.

Then
The train races
To its predestination
And the vulture
Circles home.

So
Magic lives
In a parabola of time.

Although it was
A mere stand of trees
The wilderness spoke life
In the reach
Of the everlasting
As cosmic consciousness
Spirited the moment
From the unknown.

Although the air
Carried a chill
The sun brought
A touch of warmth
As The Unknown God
Infused the moment
With blessings
A treasure
For the here and now.

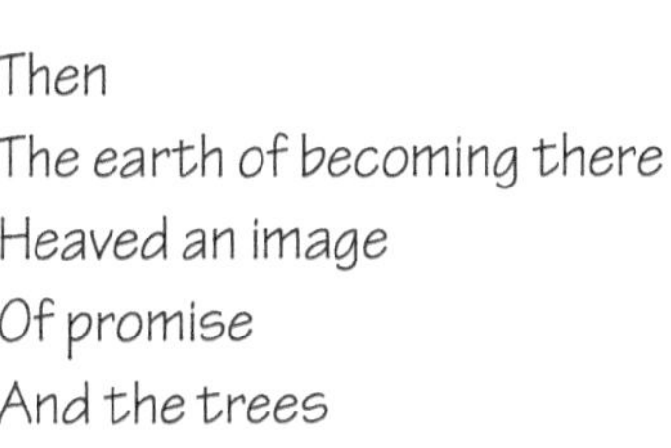

Then
The earth of becoming there
Heaved an image
Of promise
And the trees
Birthed buds of life.

Hope pictured
The blossoming of Truth
In times and a half
As the daffodils
Danced across
An old grave yard.

So
The stand of trees
Bordered the graves
With life
And the daffodils
Rejoiced in the coming
Resurrection.

Then
Hope leaped outside
Linear time
As she felt Winchester
Her muse
Embrace her substance
And passion roared
In her blood.

It was
The blaze of The Word
That trumpeted
The moment
As her two
Dimensional reality
Extracted Truth
From the living
And the dead.

How
The artist in her
Listened to The Counselor
That celebrated
Her life
And liberated her
From the second death.

As the duduk
Touched the heart
With its sorrowful song
Hope saw the dignity
Of the human spirit
Shine through time
And space.

It was
In the deep touch
Of tragedy
That a people longed

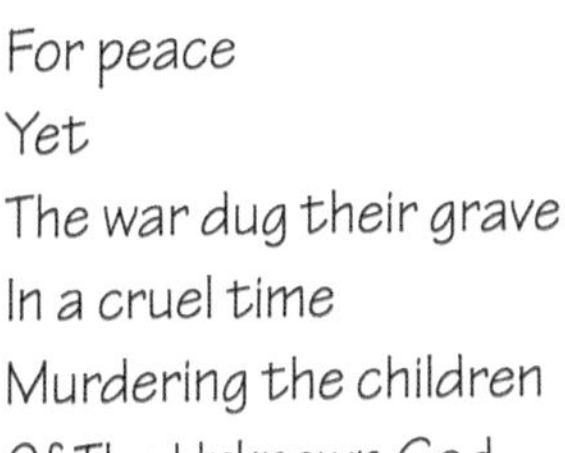

For peace
Yet
The war dug their grave
In a cruel time
Murdering the children
Of The Unknown God.

How
The forests wept
Over the brutality
Of the heartless.

How
The land raged
Over the lost blood
Yet
The Word heard
Their cry
Giving them the strength
To carry on.

To endure
How life braves
The wilds
Of the human heart
And even in darkest of times
A people find a way
To the light
Of the everlasting.

How
Faith infuses a people
With courage
So their stamina
Finds the muscle
To live.

Then
Hope takes their faces
Into a moment
Coloring the spirit
With the fortification
Of Truth.

Basking in the light
Of Truth
A people rise
From the ashes of war
Finding the peace
Beyond understanding.

Warming up
To dimensions
Of thought
Hope purged herself
Of the ways
Of the senseless round

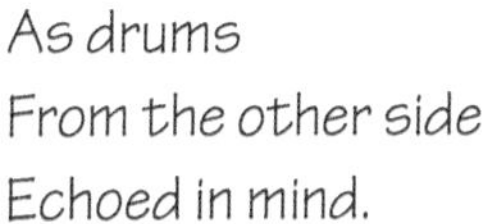

As drums
From the other side
Echoed in mind.

It was
The rhythm
Of the Deep Touch
That brought her
To an even place
And her muse
Poured passion
Into becoming there.

So
Cognition found
In a vertical column
Of time
Brought hidden meaning
Into view
As the duduk
Wept
Across the moment.

Although the secrets
Of the secrets
Of the here and now
Cloud Truth
It becomes apparent
That only
Through faith

Could the music
Of The Deep Touch
Reach the heart.

So
Hope throttled
Through barriers
Of sound
Into a portal
Leading
To the always already
There
As her muse
Marked the milestones
To Truth.

Then
Time began again
With the call of the crows.

While Hope followed
The crow
Through the wilderness
Of thought
Time and space
Aligned
With the celestial
Clocks.

It was
The movement
When time present
Enveloped
Her destiny with cosmic
Consciousness.

Then
A train depot entered
Mind
As a two dimensional
Reality
With the snow
The color
Of corpse blue
And the sky covered
Becoming there
With a shroud
Of cold grey.

Although the tracks ran
Through a destiny
Of nothingness
The sun lit
The horizon
With a wealth of gold.

How
The crow spoke Truth
Into visions

That Vashakmadze
Grasped
And linear time
Exploded
In Hope's third eye
With epiphany
After epiphany.

So
It is that Truth
Is the substance of becoming there
And the crow calls
To the heart
Through the third eye.

As time and space
Dissolve
In possibility
Hope reaches
The Deep Touch
Through faith
The connection
To The Unknown God.

It is
A matter
Of escaping self
Deception

And holding
A pure heart
And a clear mind
That allows Hope
To reach
A vertical column
Of time.

Although
Always at the edge
Of nothingness
The crow equips her
With visions far beyond
The dull round
Bringing her
To the promised land.

Then
Her muse
Infuses her
With the passion
To endure
As she fashions
A message
Of the minute
Particular.

Once there
The rhythm of the moment
Releases Truth

Through a portal
To the beyond
As the crow opens
The third eye.

So
The crow, an advisor
To this side
Of mind
Drew an image
And Hope moved
Her sights
To a man
Who lost himself
In war.

In his eyes
Was the pain
Of battle
The dead he killed
And the death
Of his buddies.

Although the war
Was in the past
He lived the brutality
Of war

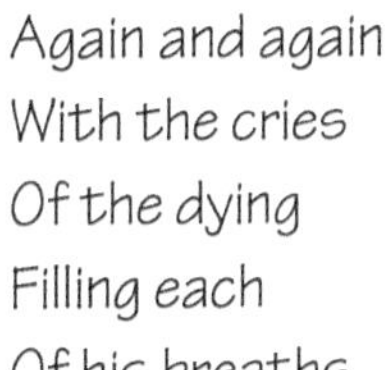

Again and again
With the cries
Of the dying
Filling each
Of his breaths.

Although
Decades had passed
His eyes reflected
The haunting of ghosts
And they were there
In his dreams
And they were there
Around every corner
Of time present.

How
Ruthless were
The memories
That paralyzed
His mind
And the crow
Wept
Over his life.

So
His life was
A living death
A dying breath.

Then
The possible
Stretched Hope Shields
Between becoming there
And the always already
There
While nothingness
Saturated the moment.

So
Time froze
As the celestial clocks
Wound down
To the abyss.

Although Hope struggled
As self churned
In silence
Her muse knelt
Before The Word
Calling
For deliverance.

Then
The house
Of many mansions
Appeared

And The Unknow God
Gave her
Blessed assurance.

It is
Because the authentic
Dwells in heart
That mind climbs
Into an atmosphere
Of Truth.

Then
Cosmic consciousness
Loaded a duduk
An overture signaling
The pain
Of what matters.

So
Shields carried on
By the power
Of The Deep Touch.

So
It was the call
Of the authentic article
That came
To becoming there

As the shadows
Of what matters
Followed the vision
Of the other side
Of a parabola of time.

To leap
Into the understanding
Of time and space
Winchester drew
Upon the war
Of being
And nothingness
And his dream
Figured the expanse
In terms
Of the here and now.

Then
Winchester read
The elements
Of the celestial clocks
Leading to the connection
Of self
To the minute particular
While the crows
Opened a corridor
To the everlasting.

How
A grain of sand
Measured the length
Of the living moment
As Winchester gathered
Time and times
And a half.

It was
The mask of the here
And now
That yielded
The mystery
Of being and time
As Winchester
Embraced
The rapture
Of his dream.

So
It was her faith
That took Winchester
Into the understanding
Of the way, the Truth
And the life
As he found
The substance
Of becoming there
In the authentic
Article.

Then
There was an old man
Sitting at a table
In Chester Park
As mind took in
The shimmering waters
As the geese
Headed south.

There is
A stand of trees there
Around a cemetery
For those long dead
Where the crows
Spread their magic.

In that moment
He recalled a dream
And she was lovely
With doe eyes
And rich auburn hair.

She was
A love of times past
An artist of Truth
And promise.

How
He thought of her
In tender moments.

She taught him
About the third eye
And the deep touch
With a wisdom
Of being and time.

Her heart was pure.

He wondered
Why they did not
Stay together.

How
His life would be
So very different
Had they stayed
Together.

In this moment
He remembered
Her substance
As an intoxicating
Fragrance.

The old man
Thought himself

Fortunate
To have known her.

As Hope slept
Each night
Her muse embraced
Her dreams
With wondrous images.

Together
They rumbled
Through time and space
Feeding
Upon beauteous treasures.

Together
They rode3 their hogs
Through the wilderness
Of thought
As their third eye
Connected to Truth.

In her dreams
They took
To being warriors
Battling against
The cruelty
Of the dull round.

Then
There were tender moments
As they tumbled
Through the passion
Of body rubbing body
As their substance
Brewed
A splendorous heat.

How
Her dreams throbbed
With the deep touch.

How
Hope gathered all
The desire
In becoming there
And her muse
Met her
With the elixir
Of the authentic
Article.

When the moment
Burst
With consummation
She smiled
Through her sigh.

Although there are
Secrets
In the here and now
The nature
Of a three dimensional reality
It is
Through the third eye
That they surfaced
As a projection
Of a parabola of time
The moment configured
In times and a half.

It is
In the darkness
Of the heart
That mystery dwells
And it blinds
Seeing the substance
Of the close at hand
Being a barrier
To what matters.

Because the mind
Is prone
To self-deception
It is
Through a two

Dimensional reality
That becoming there
Accesses Truth.

So
The artist painted
The substance
Of what was there
As an image
Beyond thought
Although it connected
To the visceral
Of being and time.

How
Hope, as the artist
uncovers
The face of Truth
Through the deep touch.

When time awakens
Into a moment
And visions yield
Images of want
How
The song

Of the everlasting
Arouses life
Into becoming there.

Then
The artist moves
Into a parabola
Of time
And heart lifts want
Into driving passion.

So
Hope reaches
Into mind
With the deep touch
As her muse
Triggers the anthem
Of Truth
And the authentic article
Dances
With forevermore.

Then
An old soldier
Bleeds life
From the pit
Of memories
And his eyes
Speak of war.

Try as he will
He cannot escape
The horror
Of battle
The cry of the dying
Echoing in mind.

Seeing Hope's smile
He remembered
The grimace of agony.

Basking in the light
Of forevermore
Hope looked
Onto the secrets
Buried in the now
As a crow took to wing
From the unknown.

Rising
From the center
Of being and time
Came a drift
Of hidden meaning
Placed
Upon the tongue
Of mind

And her muse trumpeted
The beginning
Of another moment
With The Unknown God.

Then
The crow pronounces
The authentic article
In the blood
As the bells chime
The presence
Of blessed assurance.

There is
Truth in the wind
And life
In the heart
As becoming there navigates
Through a world
Of darkness.

So
Hope carries
Her substance
Along the way
With the Deep Touch
Of The Counselor.

Then
Eternity celebrates
The age of Truth
And the age
Of forevermore.

Then
The shadow
Of a crow passes
Through the blood
Of becoming there
As Truth erases
Self-deception.

There was
A moment when
Hope triggered
Thoughts
Of the everlasting
An age loaded
With visions of substance
As the form
Of a crow launched
Mystery
Through the third eye.

So
A moment seemed
Forever
When the seeds
Of Truth
Grew into a blossoming
Of what matters
And Hope moved
Times and a half
Into the palm
At the beginning
Of mind.

Then
The wind moves
Becoming there
Into thoughts
Of a mystery tree
And the dull round
Listens
Toi the heart
Of cosmic consciousness.

How
Blind a world
Gasping for Truth
While absence is its destiny.

Then
The Word
Opens the way
To Truth
And little children
Rush
Into the arms
Of The Unknown God.

SECTION 5

Walking into Nothingness

Sitting
In the garden
Of tables and chairs
They took
To a painting
By Seurat
A beach scene
With figures all about.

Stirring
In the moment
Hope sketched
The artists feeding off
Each other
As the sun rose.

There was
Aa moment of suspension
That encompassed
Becoming there
Although mind
Anointed a character
Who looked larger
Than life.

The character's story stood
As a profile
Of time and space

Inhabited by absence
As the artists
Occupied the unknown
In search of Truth.

To build the moment
Preserved in oils
Hope read the rhythm
Of cosmic consciousness
Pulling life
Into a two-dimensional
Reality.

Then
Her muse signaled
The beginning
Of forevermore
In the bones of the artists
As they lived
A life of the calling.

How
Time past and time present
Blended together
Making a serenade
Of form and substance
Thrown into the always
Already there
Through the deep touch.

To commune
With the Deep Touch
As the moment
Rises above the sky
How
The artist configures
The physics of things
In themselves
And the essence
Of becoming there speaks
Through hidden meaning.

It is
The song
Of the mocking bird
That opens the beyond
As Hope looks
Into cosmic consciousness
Triumphing
Over the stare
Of the abyss.

Then
She reaches a soldier
Whose eyes bleed pain
And the memories
Of pain.

In his substance
Lingers
The cruel awakening
Of war.

So
As he walks
Through time and space
A vulture shadows
His mind
But Hope tugs
On his heart
With the comfort
Of a smile.

His life
Is not meaninglessness
Because his pain is true.

Divided
Between here and not here
The artist centers
On the muscle
Of what must be.

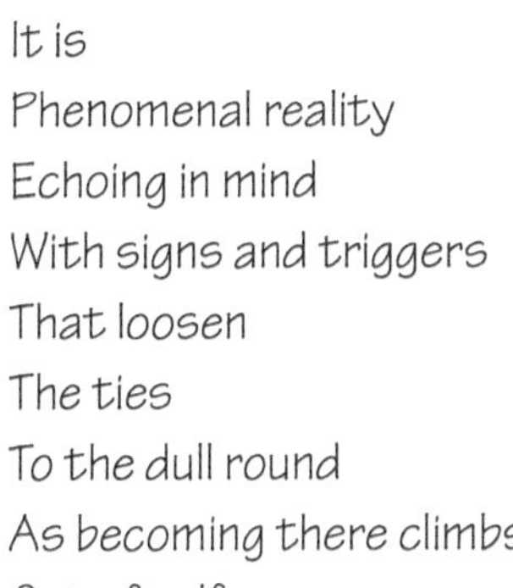

It is
Phenomenal reality
Echoing in mind
With signs and triggers
That loosen
The ties
To the dull round
As becoming there climbs
Out of self.

So
What must be
Is a vision
Of the moment
As Truth fulfills
Destiny.

So
In a one-dimensional
Reality
Time past
Time present and time future
Are one
As the cosmic clock
Encompasses
All and everything.

Then
The artist
Sees what is there

As a still life
Connected
To cosmic consciousness
Through the deep touch.

Although
The here and now
No longer exists
Hope listens to the call
Of The Unknown God
And life goes on.

An older man sat
In the garden
Of tables and chairs
Where he did
His work every day
Buying and selling homes.

It was
The way he
Afforded a good life.

His face
Narrow and long
Focused
On the immediate
As he crunched

Numbers
And weighed
The market.

His voice
Kind and gentle
Broke the silence
Of the given
As the moment
Secured his life
In becoming there.

There was
No self-deception
In his heart
And his mind
Clear
Filled time
With good thoughts.

Being a family man
As his treasure
With his children
Off to college.

The artist
Sketched him with favor
Because of his
Devotion to responsibility.

His life
Is the backbone
Of a nation.

In this vision
There was a face
Of stone
Gray in its matters.

It had
The look of eternity
In its countenanced
With no resemblance
Of a mask.

How
Truth is the substance
Dwelling in moments
And is the object
Of faith.

So
It is that the source
Of hatred is evil
Devouring
The compassionate heart
Until only nothingness
Remains.

So
Hatred poisons
The human right
To freedom
Until it becomes
Cankerous life.

How
Truth holds no hatred
But extends
The living moment
With peace
And understanding.

Then
This vision
Is the countenance
Of John the Baptist.

So
There was a young man
Who was deaf
And mute
And a holy man
Opened his ears
And fixed his voice.

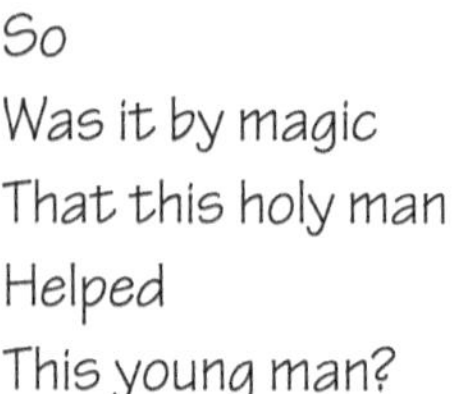

So
Was it by magic
That this holy man
Helped
This young man?

So
What is the difference
Between a magician
And a miracle man?

So
Is one
From the secular
Point of view
While the other
Is from a theological
Point of view.

So
Precisely are the magi?

Then
Winchester pulled out
Of trance
Feeling the rub
Of the cosmic clock.

Time and spacer
Filled with the deep touch
Because he had seen
The face of Truth.

Then
He had leaped
Into the beyond
Finding an understanding
Of being and nothingness
As the sky opened
With a radiant glow.

There was
A joy in his heart
As he traveled
Through time
And space.

So
The moment took him
To the other side
With his dream.

As the abyss
Carries him away
The young artist
Struggles to survive.

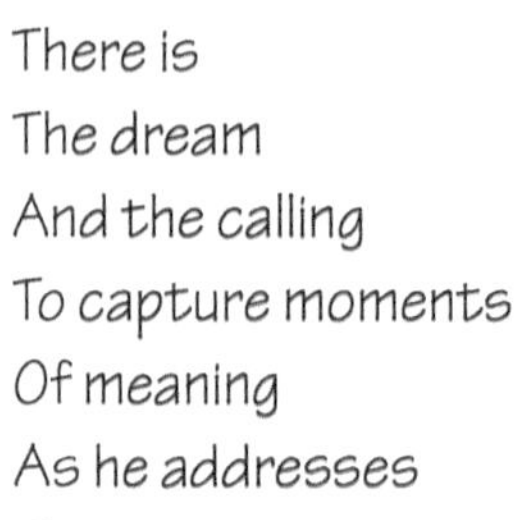

There is
The dream
And the calling
To capture moments
Of meaning
As he addresses
The canvas.

So
He raises concepts
Out of the unknown
As he sees
Only absurdity.

One question plagues him.

Why?

Abandoned by life
He faced the dull round
And it consumed him.

Although filled
With the passion
Of the artist
The void took him
Into a wasteland
Where he stumbled
Into the pit
Of despair.

Hopeless
He lingered at the edge
Of nothingness
As his spirit
Slowly died.

So
There no longer was
Light in his eyes
When he jumped
Off a bridge.

Dead.

His name
Tom Grabowski
Finds a place
In Hope's heart.

In the age
Of a lost generation
There were three
Young artists
Grabowski
Vashakmadze and Shields
And they roamed
The back roads
Of time and space.

Their spirits moved
Across being
And nothingness
As they rode
The wheels
Of ideas
Turned to images.

There was
Laughter in their bones
As good times
Gave them purpose
As they visited
The unknown
Uncovering treasures
From cosmic consciousness.

Although
Youth is a treasure
In itself
Being artists
They found gold
In their devotion
To art.

They were
Kindred spirits
On a journey
To express beauty

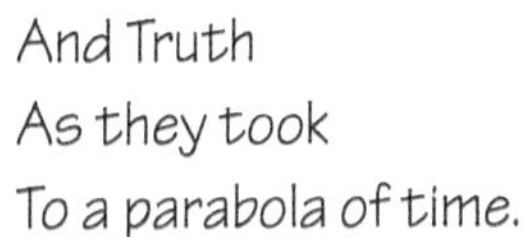

And Truth
As they took
To a parabola of time.

Then
Mind left the now
As they painted
The beyond
With the blood
Of becoming there
Their lives
A testament
To hidden meaning.

To picture
The horizon of forevermore:
Their destiny.

So
What is there
Points
To the substance
Of what matters
A moment
With The Unknown God.

So
Theophilus
As a mentor
Opened passages
To the beyond
Growing each
Of the young artists
Grabowski
Vashakmadze and Shields
Into their own self.

Each of the three
Followed their heart
To visions
That transcended
Being and time
As they reached
The deep touch
Through their own
Designs.

To express the image
Of Truth
How
They fashion moments
That picture the substance
Of things in themselves
While their gestures
Form worlds beyond thought.

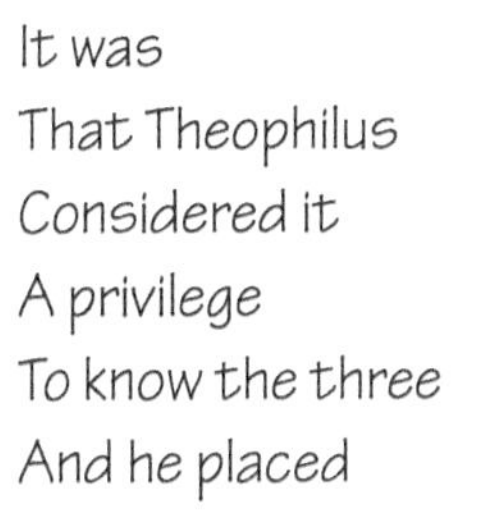

It was
That Theophilus
Considered it
A privilege
To know the three
And he placed
A trust in their art.

Then
One snowy day
Theophilus
Passed away
Leaving the three
As his legacy.

At his grave
They came with promise
In their minds
And tears
In their hearts.

So
Dr. Campbell Tatham lives on.

So
Hope Shields entered
Trance
To probe the unknown

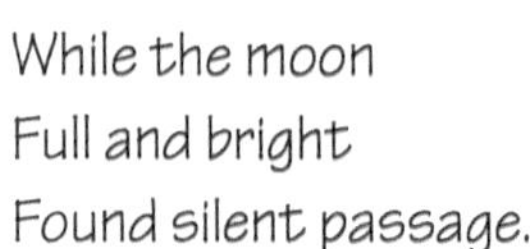

While the moon
Full and bright
Found silent passage.

Reading the signs
Of possibility
She leaped out
Of linear time
Climbing out of self
To find treasures
In cosmic consciousness.

Out of nothingness
Appeared the figure
Of an ancient man
His eyes filled
With Truth.

His reflection crossed the sky.

So
Tomorrow dawned
And the secrets
Hidden by the close
At hand
Wove a message
In mind
Gesturing toward
The Unknown God.

Then
The ancient man
Theophilus by name
Cast a shadow
In the form
Of a mystery tree.

Shields
Heard the whispering
Of thee wind
As it tossed the man's hair.

Then
His substance showed
The other side
Of time and space.

From the garden
Of tables and chairs
Hope followed
The flight
Of a hawk until
Time and space
Dissolved
Into a moment.

Then
Mind eclipsed becoming there
And Hope drank in
The substance
Of Vashakmadze's work
That carried visions
Of Truth.

Although they spun
The everlasting
As their mission
The dull round
Rejected the way
The Truth and the life
As the face
Of the celestial clocks
Marked destiny
For the living and the dead.

So
The hawk circled
The unknown
And Hope drew
The passion
Of the authentic
Article.

From somewhere
Grabowski etched
The Word

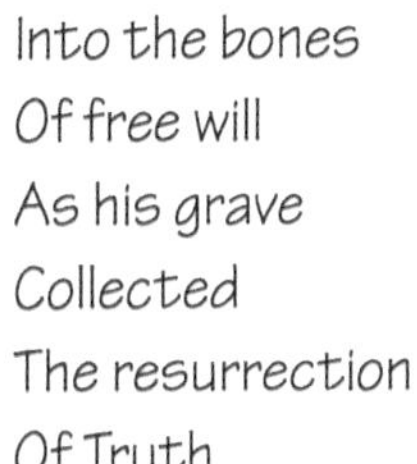

Into the bones
Of free will
As his grave
Collected
The resurrection
Of Truth.

How
Kindred spirits share
The treasures
Of forevermore.

Bones broken
Smashed skull
And Winchester rubs
Some dirt
On the pain
As he limps
To the rhythm
Of the eternal drums.

There is no
Holding him back
From his destiny
As The Unknown God
Welcomes him
To a moment.

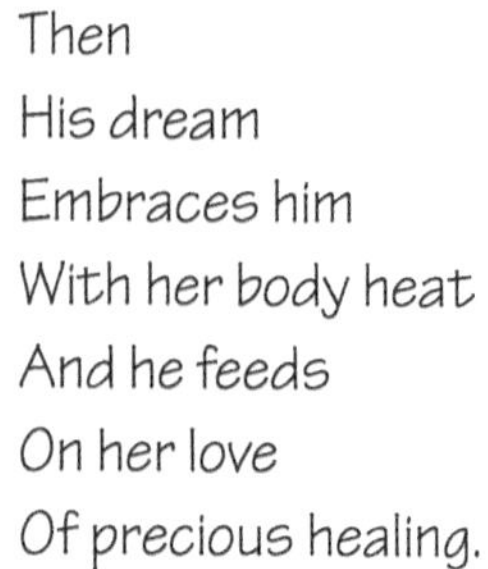

Then
His dream
Embraces him
With her body heat
And he feeds
On her love
Of precious healing.

Above
Crows take away
His pain
As his faith
Delivers him
To the deep touch.

Mounting his hog
With his dream
Holding him tightly
He follows
The call of the unknown
And the crows
Guide his breath
To the authentic article.

It is
A ride into cosmic
Consciousness
As he leaves
A two-dimensional

Reality
And he grows
Into the moment
With renewed strength.

Although time and space
Have no end
He travels
To a valley
Of dry bones
As the wind
Passes life onto them
And time past
Registers
The power of The Word.

So
Destiny makes a place
For his dream and him.

SECTION 6

Daylight in the Unknown

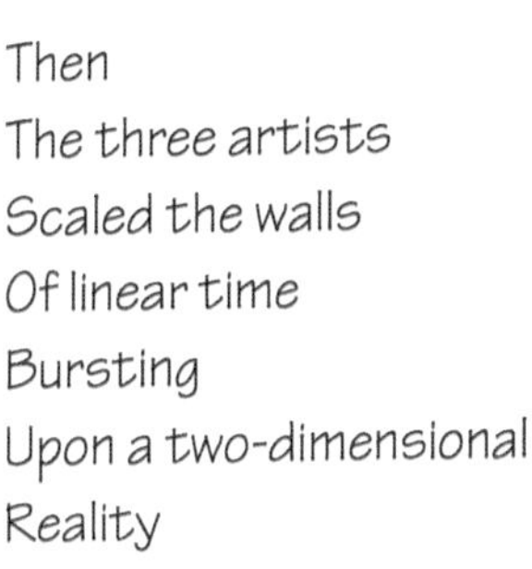

Then
The three artists
Scaled the walls
Of linear time
Bursting
Upon a two-dimensional
Reality
As The Counselor
Guided them to Truth.

It was
The language
Of hidden meaning
That they heard
As the duduk
Cried out
From the wilderness.

So
They shared the treasure
Of the moment
A moment loaded
With the doctrine
Of the landscape.

Although mind finds
The source
Of nothingness
As a thing
Born out of language

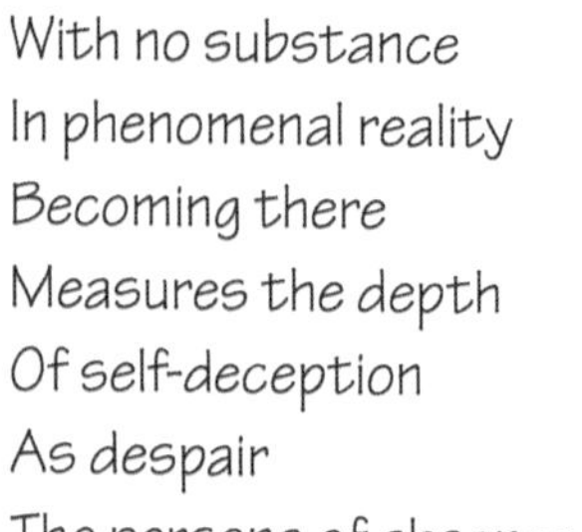

With no substance
In phenomenal reality
Becoming there
Measures the depth
Of self-deception
As despair
The persona of absence.

How
The jaws of nothingness
Devours
The substance
Of what matters
Consuming the self
Until desolation
Fills the landscape.

So
They experience
The void
As an attack
Upon the heart
Of the authentic
Article.

It is a matter
Of outliving self.

Across the expanse
Mind deciphered
The code
Of becoming there
As the artist pictured
Things in themselves
Feeding off
Of cosmic consciousness.

Then
The look
Of an old man
Presents times
And a half
As he drifts
Away from now
And enters the elements
Of the other side.

Although the form
Of what was there
Configured
The progression
Of thought
The old man
Rises from self
Into the substance
Of the moment.

How
The mystery
Of the deep touch
Moves the artist
Beneath the skin
Of the unknown
Until pure music
Overflows
And the old man
Explodes with wonder.

So
The duduk traced
A life
Across the barriers
Of time and space
And becoming there
Triumphed
Over outliving self.

Because the artist
Erased nothingness
The old man carries on.

Because a wilderness
Surrounded becoming there
Hope reached

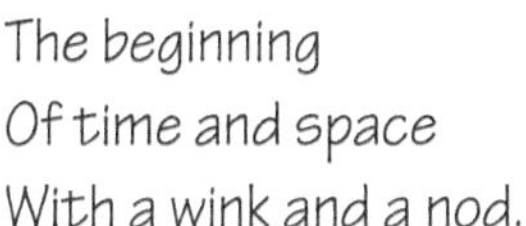

The beginning
Of time and space
With a wink and a nod.

What
Folly fills the mind
As it attempts
To reason
The dimensions
Of possibility.

Then
Hope pictured
The moment
When vertical time
Birthed
A three-dimensional
Reality.

So
It is through
The Unknown God
That a vision
Appears
A vision of the house
Of many mansions
The origin
Of all and everything.

There
Beyond time and space
Beyond possibility
And beyond thought
Grows the seed
Of what matters
And al of linear time
Becomes
A grain of sand.

So
Hope found purpose
In cosmic consciousness
The Counselor
And the domain
Of the Word
Where Truth lives
Always and forever.

How
The heart cries out
When the crows
No longer visit
Becoming there
And mind find
Itself a prisoner
Of the dull round.

It is
That they carry
The artist
Into the substance
Of phenomenal reality
Where the muscle
Of purpose
Pumps life into life.

Because they know
The way
To the other side
Hope cherishes
The moments
That they bring
Moments of basking
In the light
Of cosmic consciousness.

Then
A mocking bird
Signals
The return of Truth
A song
Of joy and wonder
That unchains
Free will.

So
The artist
Unearths hidden meaning
With the deep touch
As crows
Come to life in the mind.

How
The thought of crows
Awakens
Becoming there to Truth.

So
The crows play
In a golden field.

Van Gogh knew it well.

Although
He was the general's
Favorite corporal
He knew
The wasteland
He knew
The mutilation of life
He lived through
The War in Vietnam.

How
He remembered
The smell of death.

So
The old man lived
His face
A testament
To tortuous pain
That rotted his heart.

No longer was there
Light in his eyes.

So
He went the way
Of the living dead
As his shadow
Haunted him
As he marched
Into the abyss.

In his look
He sought the horizon
Searching for something
To give him peace.

Some wounds never heal.

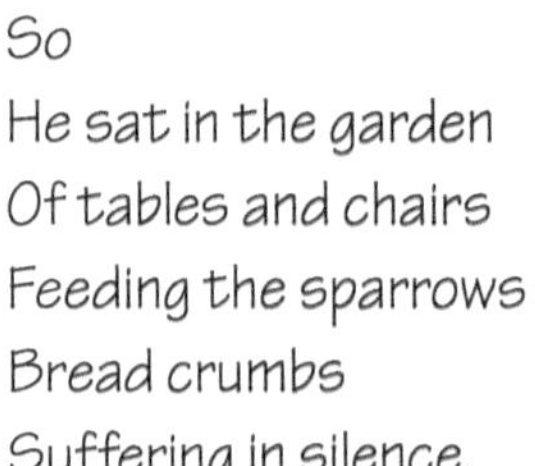

So
He sat in the garden
Of tables and chairs
Feeding the sparrows
Bread crumbs
Suffering in silence.

To be hopeless: how sad.

So
There was a sign
In the bones
Of becoming there
That the time
Drew near when the blood
Returned to eternity.

Then
The crows gathered
In his mind
And Winchester
Turned
To a two-dimensional
Reality
Looking to the stars
For the portal
To cosmic consciousness.

Pounding the pavement
With his hog
He felt the deep touch
Of his dream
As she poured
Passion
Into his heart.

She is
The encompassing
Of wonder
And he is
The breath
Of the wilds.

Then
The sky pronounced
Life
Into his self
As eons of time past
Flowed
Into the moment.

It was
A look into a one
Dimensional reality
That delivered them
Onto Truth
And The Unknown God
Spoke

To his heart
With the hope
Of the everlasting.

So
The trumpet sounded
And the heavens opened
As The Word
Called the moment
Into forevermore.

Then
Winchester and his dream
Were given the peace
Beyond understanding.

How
The mountains break
The horizon
As the valley defines
Time and space.

There is no
Other side
Of the close at hand
But the interminable
Unknown.

How
Safe this place is
While the edge
Of mind
Stays in the shallows
Of being and time.

To wear
The mask of the here
And now
How
Moments of Truth
Focuses
Visions of eternity.

Then
There are Winchester
And his dream
Who venture
Through the unknown
Onto the wonders
Of the wilderness
And the physics
Of becoming there.

So
The Unknown God
Guides them
Through the shadows
Of nothingness

Filling them
With the courage
To be
With the living moment
And to gather
The Truth
Of cosmic consciousness.

Then
They follow
The call of The Word
As Winchester
Presses
Into the beyond
And his dream
Fills him
With what matters
As she deciphers
The message
Of the deep touch.

Without The Word
There would be
The abyss for them
Only.

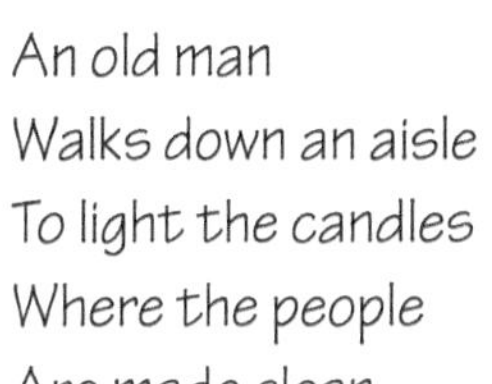

An old man
Walks down an aisle
To light the candles
Where the people
Are made clean.

It is not
What is beyond them
But what has been
Given to them
From beyond
That works the miracle
Of redemption.

To believe as a child
How time past
Is redeemed
By the blood
Of the lamb
And the old man
Passes
A reverent eye
Across time and space.

Either
One answers the call
To believe
Or one turns away
From The Unknown God

As The Word
Offers the deep touch
For all.

So
Some have a heart
Of stone
And a mind
That is deaf
To the call to faith
Yet
The Spirit of Truth
Is there always
Ready for the ear
To hear
And the heart
To hold fast
To the precious faith.

It is
That in linear time
The call
Is always already there
While in a vertical column
Of time
The Unknown God
Predestines believers.

So
In linear time
There is hope
To answer the call.

Tragic it is
That some do not listen
In days of becoming.

So
The mountains hide
In the fog
And the here and now
Disappear.

There is
Only the moment
As Winchester leaves
What is there
For a parabola of time
His trance
Taking mind
Into the other side.

He is
A still life
Of form and substance
As his dream

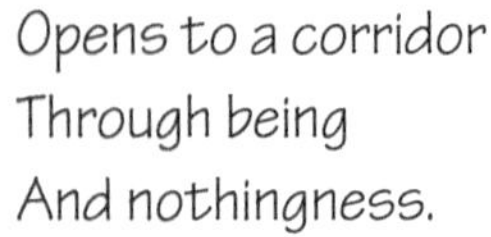

Opens to a corridor
Through being
And nothingness.

Then
Thought searches
The unknown
For the deep touch
As his dream
Takes the persona
Of being and time
Into moments
Of the everlasting.

So
There is the third eye
That probes
What is there
Supplying an understanding
Of the physics
Of time and space
As the knowing
Of Truth
Reveals faith
In The Unknown God.

Centering himself
On the essence
Of his dream
Winchester leaps

Into the wonder
Of The Word
As he fastens himself
To the core
Of becoming there.

So
All of this is
An echo
Of cosmic consciousness
And the celestial clocks
Mold his destiny
As a witness
To Truth.

So
Winchester experiences
The God Particle
Through the bread
And wine
Of The Word.

Within the encompassing
And through the cosmic clock
The Unknown God
Cares for the children
Of promise

As eons
And worlds beyond worlds
Define the moment.

It is
The faith
In The Word that redeems
Time past
As self gathers
The wisdom of the ages.

Then
Winchester turns
To his dream
As she breathes
Eternity
Into the moment.

How
Love conquers despair
As a moment
With The Unknown God
Liberates becoming there
From the bondage
Of self-deception.

To open
The eyes of becoming
Winchester finds
Freedom

In the archeology
Of time and space
And his dream
Sings beauty
Into the flesh
Of what matters.

Advancing
Into meditation
Winchester sees
The close at hand
As the finger prints
Of The Unknown God
And his dream
Carries him
Into the communion
With kindred spirits.

So
Life with The Word
Issues the message
Of peace on earth
And good will
To all.

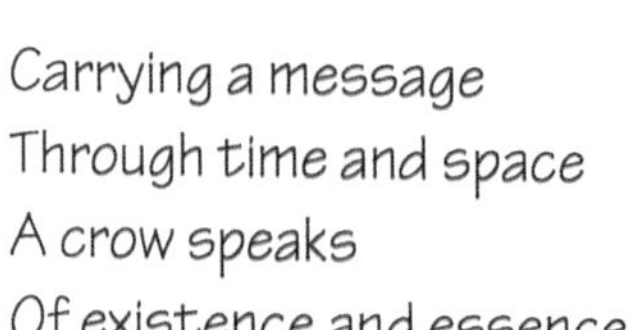

Carrying a message
Through time and space
A crow speaks
Of existence and essence,

To be
In the frontier
Of being and nothingness
How
The message reveals
The characters
Of hidden meaning.

Then
The dream
Of Winchester
Defines the moment
As entrance
Into the beyond.

Once there
She nourishes
Out living self
With Truth
And becoming there grows
Into the authentic
Article.

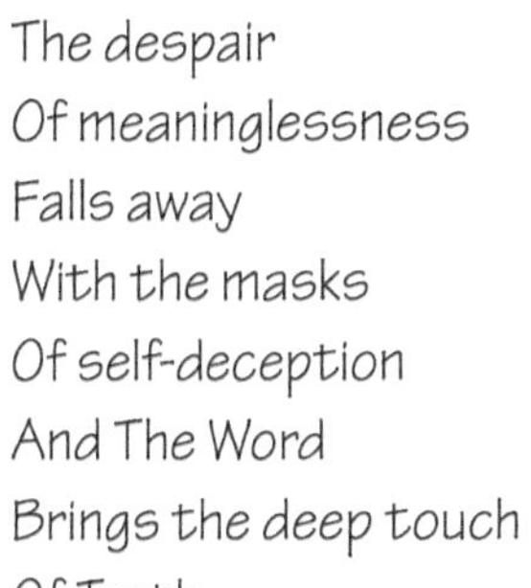

The despair
Of meaninglessness
Falls away
With the masks
Of self-deception
And The Word
Brings the deep touch
Of Truth.

How
The message
Of cosmic consciousness
Liberates mind
From bondage.

Then
Winchester follows
The crow
Through a corridor
Of time
As space configures
A two-dimensional
Reality.

So
The substance
Of becoming there speaks
The language

Of essence
And the architecture
Of the close at hand
Defines the form
Of existence.

Without existence
There is no platform
For doing.

Without substance
Life is a shallow grave.

There is
A look in her eyes
As she configures
A dream
For Winchester
A dream of magic
And a dream of mystery.

She
Opens the sky
With the pursuit
Of hidden meaning
As the stars

Weave a tapestry
Of moments
In time and times
And a half.

Then
The wilderness
Turns golden
As the day passes
Into eternity
And the rub
Of autumn Impassions
The will to be.

In his core
Winchester reaches the ends
Of thought
As the beginning
Of new horizons
Makes visions dance
To the drums
Of eternity.

How
The third eye
Delivers the moment
When he feels
The dynamic

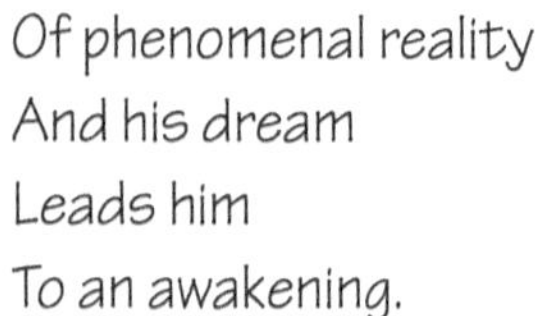

Of phenomenal reality
And his dream
Leads him
To an awakening.

Truth rises from there
As a one-dimensional
reality
Allows the coalescing
Of understanding
As his dream
Feeds him
With the visions
Of forevermore.

So
They turn to The Word
For the will
Of cosmic consciousness
The Being of Truth.

So
Truth is the essence
Of The Unknown God
And is perceived
Through the third eye
As belief

Is the threshold
That allows adoption
Into the always already
There.

So
Winchester rides
His hog
Into the wilderness
Of time and space
With faith
In The Word
To keep him away
From self-deception.

On the road
Exploring ideation
He holds fast
To the substance
Of becoming there
As he searches
Through the living
Moment.

At times
His faith is solid
While at other times
His faith wavers
Like a candle
In the wind.

He is a seeker
Of Truth
And the way of Truth.

How
Mind hungers for rest
As he rides
Being driven
By an insatiable desire
For what matters most.

There is
A hidden meaning
In time and space
Found only
Through the deep touch
Of cosmic consciousness
And The Word
Gives him comfort
Through the love
Of his dream.

Then
As he journeys
Through the abyss
His pursuit of Truth
Is his destiny.

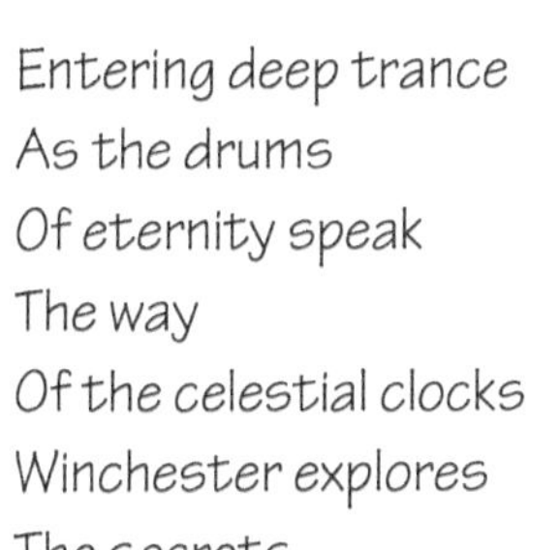

Entering deep trance
As the drums
Of eternity speak
The way
Of the celestial clocks
Winchester explores
The secrets
Of hidden meaning
Through the projection
Of will.

Everywhere
There is the unknown
A jungle
Of things-in-themselves
Attacking mind.

To
Leave the chaos
Winchester leap
Into a two-dimensional
Reality
And becomes
A self-portrait
In a still life.

There
He sees
Through the window
Of the always

Already there and ignites
The thoughts of time
And times and a half.

Then
There is a clearing
Where mind
Holds a mystery
Of crystal
Because he passed
Through the barriers
Of linear time.

It is
That the abyss
Occupies becoming there
With shadows
Of self-deception
As he tangles
In outliving-self.

So
He projects himself
Into the presence
Of The Word
And life turns
Into la luscious garden
Where peace
And understanding
Beat the drums
Of forevermore.

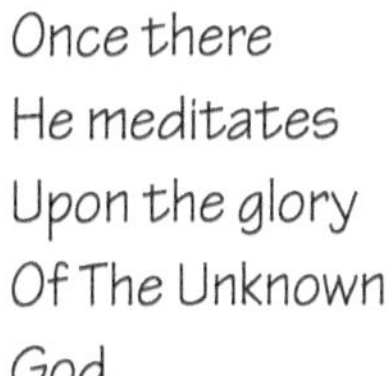

Once there
He meditates
Upon the glory
Of The Unknown
God.

When worlds collide
And the fires
Of desperation
Burn out of control
It is time
For fight or flight.

How
The heart aches
For peace
But the surroundings
Disrupt mind
With chaos.

There is no
Easy way
Out of the abyss.

Then
Winchester levels
His load

With both barrels
Filled
With hot lead.

The only way
Through
Is to let blood run.

Anger.

Then
From beyond
A feeling reaches
Into his core
And Winchester
Gets a grip.

Trancing
Out of the now
Where the moment
Is filled
With acid air
Winchester breathes in
Comfort
From The Word.

How
Cruel the moment was
As anger took
Control

But
The Unknown God
Turned
Time and times
And a half
Into a moment
Of Truth.

So
Winchester built
A moment
Of reflection
Finding hope
In The Word.

To live
In the mountains
Where the splendor
Of becoming there
Trumpets the moment
How
The heart rejoices.

There is
A music in the wilderness
That fills the heart
With magic

As time and times
And a half
Issue the birth
Of forevermore.

So
The Tennessee River
Winds
Through eternity
Reflecting the brilliance
Of The Unknown God
And Hope gathers
The treasures
Of immortality.

Then
Winchester lives on.

Then
He mounts his hog
And rides
With his dream
Hope
Into the starry night.

So
A crescent moon
Guides them
Into the way
The Truth and the life

As he throttles
Through time and space.

How
The moment
Of ecstasy feeds them
With wonder.

How
They rumble
Through the wilds
Following an epiphany
Of grace.

So
His Hope
His dream come true
Opens a vision
Of what matters
As they turn
To The Word
In the living moment.

To transcend
Time and space
To see what is there
How
The third eye

Equips becoming there
With the vision
Of the everlasting.

So
The artist in Hope Shields
Massages the moment
Until her passion
Over comes
The close at hand
And she visits
The rub
Of venturous times.

Then
The duduk forms
An interlude
When the mystery
Of the beyond
Saturates
The flesh of beauty
And Truth.

With the pallet
Of the authentic article
She configures
A milestone, a step
Into things in themselves
And the image

Suspends the domain
Of thought.

Because
The unknown unfolds
Into a song
The hymn
Of the everlasting
The power
Of The Counselor
Speaks
Into the heart
Of becoming there.

Then
The Unknown God
Breathes life
Into the moment
And Hope
Believes herself
Into the other side
Of time and space.

So
There is mystery
In the flesh
And magic in the bone

As the moment
Takes Hope Shields
Into the inside
Of becoming there.

Because the substance
Of phenomenal reality
Pulls her ever closer
To the deep touch
She stretches
Time and space
Into the image
Of the unknown.

Then
The artist in her
Reveals
The hidden meaning
In a wilderness
Of thought.

How
Cosmic consciousness
Feeds here
With the authentic article
As she faces
Nothingness
With the sabre

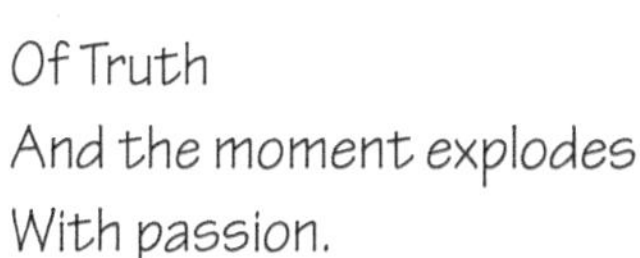

Of Truth
And the moment explodes
With passion.

It is
Her bond
With her mentor
That eclipses
The heart
Of what is there
Until she grasps
The beyond
With the power
Of always and forever.

Then
She becomes the light
Of pure music.

www.ingramcontent.com/pod-product-compliance
Lightning Source LLC
Chambersburg PA
CBHW032218050726
47591CB00001B/169